# *Let's* DECORATE

## *By* Laurence Llewelyn-Bowen

LET'S DECORATE

By Laurence Llewelyn-Bowen

First Published in North America in 2010 by
CREATIVE HOMEOWNER®
Upper Saddle River, NJ 07458

# CRE▲TIVE
## HOMEOWNER®

Creative Homeowner® is a registered trademark of Federal Marketing Corporation.

First published in the United Kingdom by Quadrille in 2010 as
*Decorating with Laurence Llewelyn-Bowen*
Quadrille Publishing Limited
Alhambra House, 27-31 Charing Cross Road,
London WC2H 0LS
www.quadrille.co.uk

Editorial Director: Anne Furniss
Creative Director: Helen Lewis
Art Director: Gabriella Le Grazie
Design Concept: Llewelyn-Bowen Limited
Project Editor: Simon Davis
Photography: Polly Wreford, Carolyn Barber
Production Vincent: Smith, Marina Asenjo
Editorial Assistant: Sarah Jones

**Creative Homeowner**
VP/Publisher: Timothy O. Bakke
Managing Editor: Fran J. Donegan
Art Director: David Geer
Senior Editor: Kathie Robitz
Junior Editor: Angela Hanson
Production Coordinator: Sara M. Markowitz
Photo Coordinator: Mary Dolan
Digital Imaging Specialist: Frank Dyer

Current Printing (last digit)
10 9 8 7 6 5 4 3 2 1

Let's Decorate!, First Edition
Library of Congress Control Number: 2010923022
ISBN 10: 1-58011-508-X
ISBN 13: 978-1-58011-508-7

CREATIVE HOMEOWNER®
A Division of Federal Marketing Corp.
24 Park Way
Upper Saddle River, NJ 07458
**www.creativehomeowner.com**

## Planet Friendly Publishing
✓ Made in the United States
✓ Printed on Recycled Paper
Text: 10%    Cover: 10%
Learn more: www.greenedition.org

**GREEN EDITION**

# CONTENTS

# $\mathcal{D}$ESIGNER INSIDER

# BEING YOUR OWN INTERIOR DESIGNER

DIY doesn't just stand for "do it yourself"; it can also mean "design it yourself." This is where the real fun is—the opportunity to make your own mark on a space.

## CREATING A DESIGN SCHEME

When people ask me where they should start designing their room, I often suggest they begin with a cold glass of chardonnay. Though this advice may sound flippant, there is a point to it—at this first stage of the design process it is important that you are as relaxed and as unconstrained as possible. Spend time building up a mental picture of your own fantasy room; the more you think through a scheme, the better it becomes. By the time I hit the drawing board, I like to feel that the whole thing has been more or less entirely thought through in my head.

To create your dream room, you will need to assemble some inspiration. At this stage, try to keep it as broad as possible. If something appeals, then photograph it or tear it out of a magazine. A refrigerator, a color, a tropical island, or a pattern on a couture dress—some of the most unexpected things can provide you with that potentially highly creative starting point.

Once you have assembled images for what is known in the trade as a "sample board," put them together on a piece of foam-core presentation board. The images don't need to be arranged in orderly fashion, the point is to see whether any particular combination stands out. You may well find that one image next to a picture of something completely different suddenly ignites that spark of inspiration and, presto, a creative idea is born.

Now start collating that creative freedom into something more structured. With your empty room firmly fixed in your mind, try painting it in imaginary colors with imaginary treatments for the walls. Play around with different floor ideas. All the while you should keep relating back to your sample board for inspiration.

## GO SHOPPING

Well, at least go window shopping. Narrow down your choices to specific products. Start collating a visual presentation with samples and photographs of specific items. Keep your search broad—you do not have to be overly practical while you have your creative hat on, so don't drop that sofa just because of its king's-ransom-sized price tag. At this stage stay as loyal as you can to the creative idea. The budget will have its sway later, but not just yet.

## WRITE A TO-DO LIST

Write a list of what needs to be done. Start with the big stuff like building work or major interior carpentry; then make headings to include all the other bits and pieces—plumbing, electrical, flooring, decorating, soft furnishings, upholstery, and the fabulous "FFF" (furniture, fittings, and furnishing). Though it may not sound enthralling, there is a lot of pleasure to be had in getting this list right. Try to keep the proposed scheme at the front of your mind as you start imagining the new elements in your blank-canvas room arriving one by one. As you do, check that everything is in the right place: if you want to put the television in that corner, is there a cable connection and an electrical outlet nearby? If you put the sofa under that window, will it block the view or, more positively, will it hide that radiator?

## CREATE A SAMPLE BOARD

As your choices become more finely honed, start working up the level of detail in your design scheme. Your sample board should now have a sample or a picture of everything you are planning to do. For every product that you have chosen for your room, include as much detail as possible. So where your to-do list says "paint the ceiling," note the paint color and put in details of the supplier; where it says "lay the carpet," give all the necessary reference numbers to ensure the right carpet arrives.

## BUDGETING

Now add up your budget—yes, the scary part. The reason you've been so solicitous with your design is so that should you suddenly decide you cannot afford it all at once, at least you'll have a fixed design goal to aim for as you implement the elements piecemeal. Your considered design will also keep up your confidence as you go through the process of transforming your room. One of the worst things you can do is to run out of steam halfway through and suddenly decide that the wall color is too dark or that the carpets are too frantically patterned. Remember that all of the elements are there to work in combination, as a team. Singly and out of context, they may very well seem incoherent, but when balanced by all the ingredients in your design, they will be just what the room needs.

And even when the budget manages to break its own boundaries, try to keep the ideas contained within your design sacrosanct. So if the original sofa, with its luxurious fabric, is way too expensive, perhaps a plainer, cheaper sofa with a few big cushions in the same fabric could achieve the same effect. That wallpaper that you have chosen may cost a lot, but have you thought about rolling up your sleeves and making something similar yourself with a stencil? I can honestly say that creativity can get you out of some seemingly insurmountable budgeting tight spot. As long as you have a detailed design and sample board from which to work, you will be fine.

# Practical design

I resent interiors that turn their owners into slaves. What looks jaw-dropping in a glossy interior-design magazine may require a cadre of hired help to maintain. It is also worth remembering that nothing is immune to getting old: it is called entropy and is inescapable. A sensible mindset, then, is to focus on design schemes that tend to age gracefully.

*Choose easy-to-clean (or at least easy-to-change)* Large expanses of glass may seem marvelously modern, but they will need a lot of elbow grease to keep them looking good. When choosing paint, remember that easily repainted latex is often the most practical solution.

*Go mid-tone* Very dark or very light colors show age far worse than mid-tone shades.

*Camouflage wear and tear* Pattern is a great way of distracting the eye away from damage.

*Choose darker flooring* Floor coverings start "shadowing" after a few years of use, so work out where the heavy-traffic areas are and choose dark or mid-tone shades accordingly.

*Ventilate* Keep bathrooms and kitchens well-ventilated to protect finishes against damage.

# SPACE

It is very rare to meet someone who feels that his or her home is the perfect size. Often he or she will have a long list of gripes about it. There are too few bedrooms; the kitchen isn't big enough to swing a small cat; or the children don't have the space they need to run around inside when it rains, for example.

And yet, for all these complaints relating to size, in my experience it is the aesthetics of the home that will often tip the balance from "house love" to "house hate." While we can usually accommodate the practically imperfect, we are far harder on those spaces that, just by looking at them, give that overwhelming yet intangible feeling of gloomy depression. The architectural personality of a room has a powerful but often unremarked influence on your state of mind. Your eye might get snagged on the showy things—the colors, the accessories, and the furniture—but ultimately if the room feels wrong, you feel wrong in it. Yet admitting that a room is fundamentally the wrong shape sounds terminal; without full-scale architectural remodeling, surely the space is a write-off, isn't it?

Not so. Just as clever dressing can distract the eye from a long list of bodily imperfections, so interior decoration has some wonderfully clever tricks up its wizard's sleeve of makeover.

## CUTTING CORNERS

Luckily for us decorators, the human eye has a very turbulent relationship with the brain, which (bless it) is prone to making mistakes when assessing space. From experience, the brain knows that to get a handle on the space it needs to know where the corners are. So it sends a message to the eye to find the darkish upright lines it has come to trust as being the visual signposts to the perimeter. If the eye cannot find these signposts, then the brain sloppily presumes the room is much bigger. And that, ladies and gentleman, is the single most important thing you need to remember!

So, given that your room is likely to come complete with corners (and that you are very unlikely to be able to remove them), what is to be done? The best way to make those corners disappear is by making an eye-catching fuss of the space between them. The magpie brain cannot help but be captivated by this, trapped in the middle and blithely uninterested in the edges. This most simple and effective decorating trick does not just apply to walls—floor space can also be made to look far more generous by painting the baseboard the same color as the floor, while the installation of an eye-catching statement chandelier will transform your ceiling into an immense tundra of uninhabited space.

## USING STRIPES TO STRETCH A SPACE

It may or may not surprise you to learn that the "vertical lines elongate, horizontal lines broaden" rule that we all apply to ourselves when dressing also relates to the proportions of rooms. The key to making short, dumpy rooms feel tall and willowy is to remember to sprinkle verticals, such as full-length curtains; long, thin panels; or even graciously leggy standard floor lamps, wherever you can. Not only do these upright lines help stretch the room's proportions vertically, but their sheer number also catches the eye and makes those annoying corners even more difficult to spot. Likewise, when used cleverly in a room, broad horizontal emphasis can makes a space appear twice the width it really is.

# Room layouts

Getting the layout of a room right is a careful balance between practicality and aesthetics. Personally, I like a room to both look sensational and be functional, which for me, means that everything has a preordained place where it works best.

## LIVING ROOMS

*L-shaped works best* These days so many of our living rooms use the TV as a focal point. Often the principal visual axis runs straight from the most comfortable sofa to the TV screen, which can be difficult in rooms originally built around the warm amber glow of the fireplace. Modern solutions involving major architectural intrusion are all well and good, but the simplest solution is to create an L-shaped seating arrangement—with one sofa favoring the fireplace and another favoring the television.

## BEDROOMS

*Don't be a wallflower* There's always space for a little creativity when it comes to bedroom layouts, so don't feel tied to the walls. If there's room, putting the bed in the middle of the space can look very grand. Make sure there is a headboard so that the pillows don't keep falling off the end, and consider a piece of furniture, such as a table or desk at the foot of the bed to finish off the whole thing.

## KITCHENS

*Put the "home" into home kitchen* An unloved haven in which the cook is intended to slave away was a hundred years ago. These days the kitchen is an incredibly important room that must be the kind of space in which we can live as well as cook. I love kitchens that feel integrated into the rest of the home—with lamps on the work surfaces for gentle mood lighting, and pictures and wallpaper on the walls. If at all possible, I try also to avoid wall-hung cabinets, which always feel heavy and create a claustrophobic effect. I know you've got to keep them tidy, but using open shelves dramatically increases the feeling of space and light within a room.

# RHYTHM AND CONTRAST

Once you have opened up the box of interior-design tricks and have transformed some of those spatial wrongs into proportional rights, your room will need a bit of finessing. A bit of civilizing, if you like. You'll also want to create emphasis in certain places, to generate interest and to make features out of particular elements within a room. To achieve both these goals, an understanding of the concepts of rhythm and contrast is essential.

## RHYTHM

When you see pictures of extraordinarily beautiful rooms from the past, one of the key ingredients of their glamor is one of the most difficult things to spot. Unless, that is, you know where to look. Rhythm has a huge influence on interiors, but when it is done properly, it becomes more or less entirely invisible.

We like rhythm—it is good for the soul. Neurological experiments have proved time and again that measured, elegant rhythm spreads waves of pleasure through the brain. It is as if we love to know what's coming next: left, right, left, right, left. (And isn't it wonderful to feel safe in the knowledge that right comes next?) We like the security of understanding past, present, and future; which is why wall, curtain, window, curtain, wall, curtain, window, curtain breeds a sense of comfortable familiarity.

## SYMMETRY AND BALANCE

Rhythm at its simplest and most efficient, symmetry delights us. We see ourselves as symmetrical and love it when our environments reflect our proportions.

Arrangements of pairs, using twos, fours, or eights, all create a pleasant sense of visual harmony. The danger with a room that is too symmetrical, however, is that it can easily degenerate into a space without energy. By contrast the asymmetrical forces an instant reaction from us—symmetry lulls us into a sense of soft-focus security; a lack of symmetry wakes us up with a bang.

So, is there, out there, a midpoint between the sensible, ordered world of the symmetrical and the wild pagan bacchanalia of modernist asymmetry? There is, and it is called "balance." Using different objects to balance either side of an invisible center line is a best-of-both-worlds alternative. As an exercise, it requires everything to be seen in terms of visual weight: the more eye-catching an object, the heavier it is. So a particular "look-at-me" fireplace in stainless steel would need several much smaller framed prints hung as a unit opposite to create equilibrium.

## CONTRAST

Contrast livens up a space, but how do you go about bringing it into your scheme? First, select the element of your room that you would like to feature. Then treat it in the opposite way to its neighbors. So, if you want the eye to be immediately drawn to a centrally placed fireplace, why not wallpaper it? Or should you want to make a huge fuss of one shiny wall, why not try surrounding it with three matte walls? Color can also be a very effective way of providing contrast; while a beige suede sofa standing on a beige fitted carpet has little impact, making that sofa a shiny red creates contrast and makes for a far more theatrical statement.

# The feature wall

The concept of contrast is best seen in the use of the feature wall—painting, papering, or treating one wall in a way that is more eye-catching than that of its three neighbors.

## Choosing the right wall

Feature walls can carry a heavy price; if done wrong, they can totally overbalance a once-pleasant room. The optical science behind the feature wall theory is pretty straightforward—make one wall so eye-catching that the other three recede. But choose the wrong wall at your peril! In a long narrow room, the end wall, the wall furthest from you, is an ideal case for the feature wall. Treated differently, it will march bombastically forward, squaring off the space and killing off the room's corridor-like proportions. But should you do the same to one of the side walls, or worse still both of them, the room will become a vice—and you'll feel squeezed in the middle of it. Bringing walls forward at the room's narrowest point in this way is a work of true folly.

# COLOR

If architecture is the intellect of a room, color is its emotion. It is also the first thing we notice about any interior. We all have favorite colors (and indeed least favorite ones, too). None of us can look at a color without it's unleashing all sorts of wonderful prejudices and preconceptions.

All of this makes inheriting somebody else's color scheme far more difficult than being left with their interior layout. It also makes the act of choosing colors a little bit like walking through an imaginary minefield—with bad taste set to blow up in your face at any moment. So how should you begin? The good news is that colors are less fashionable than they used to be. There was a time when the "taste makers" would decree a particular shade as "in," thereby ensuring any other color was "out." With the democratization of taste, there is no one to say that you cannot have a lilac bedroom or a brown sitting room, should you wish. While trends in color do still exist (and flicking through this book it occurred to me that I certainly have a favorite palette that crops up a lot), as a professional interior designer I think it's really important that the lid to the paint can stays open and that colors I may have dismissed in the past get a second chance if they suit the room and the client.

## COMBINING COLORS

An ability to put colors together is often treated with mystical awe. While putting colors next to one another is not easy (and isn't helped by the fact that preference is so subjective) there are a few lessons that help. One of the most basic is the kindergarten concept of complementary colors. On the color wheel, if you remember, there are three primary colors—red, blue, and yellow. From these a group of secondary colors —green, orange, and purple—are created by mixing. And then, spreading out like a very colorful snowflake, infinite combinations create infinite colors. Pinks, turquoises, browns, grays, terra-cottas—all the shades that you could possibly imagine.

When it comes to complementary colors, opposites attract—repulsively or pleasingly depending on your point of view. Putting green next to red will intensify both, creating an energetic crescendo of color. If you are a real colorphile then remember—fortune favors the brave! Societies like those of southern India, where color is highly valued, use a number of these high-octane primary color combinations—red and green, blue and yellow, and purple and orange. Likewise the Victorians loved to squeeze every last atom out of color—as shown by the red and green combinations, which they used to breathe new life into the Scottish tartan industry.

## COLORS THAT GO

I cannot bear it when people say that colors "go." It's not just a case of semantics; I think it puts people in completely the wrong frame of mind, leading them to expect a color scheme to somehow energetically propel itself towards them. Instead, I prefer to say that colors "rhyme." This implies a color relationship that has a subtle and subjective ability to grow more attractive through familiarity, rather than the definitive "yes" or "no" implied by "go." One exercise that really helps when it comes to finding colors that co-exist well is to stop thinking of them purely visually and to start transposing them into other senses instead. Though it may sound strange, imagining colors as flavors (citrus-y limes and yellows for example) can really help to give you a fresh new perspective on color choice and is a technique that I have often found to be very successful.

## STUCK IN NEUTRAL

The late-twentieth century was definitively the age of beige. Before then, no one would have dreamt of using such a colorless color. Beige and all its neutral friends— taupe, string, straw, magnolia, and white chocolate—suited the mood of a new, energetically democratic era that was extremely self-conscious about taste and class. Somehow neutrals showed you to be, well, neutral: neither fish nor fowl, neither pretentiously posh nor aggressively crude. My sincere hope is that as we all grow in confidence we can start to explore and enjoy color again, if for no other reason than because getting a beige color scheme to work is horrendously difficult. All too often I have seen color schemes that end up as clashing mushes of euphemistic neutrals. Though beige and taupe might seem politely quiet, they can actually clash very noisily indeed.

## COLOR AND DISTANCE

Next time you're in an art gallery, have a very close-up look at an Impressionist painting. There are just two things you have to remember about the Impressionists— they painted *en plein aire* (outdoors in front of the thing they wanted to paint), and they never used black. So just how did they get that sense of distance into their wonderful landscapes? Well, rather than using tone, they used hue. They noticed that if they painted far distant mountains blue, gray, lilac, or even sometimes pink, and used reds, browns, and dark purples in the foreground, for example, they were able to achieve a pronounced sense of recession; those mountains really did seem much farther away.

If cool colors can make painted mountains feel farther away, then it only takes a small logical leap to realize that the same shades can help make the walls of your room feel that little bit more distant. In contrast, reds, browns, deep oranges, and purples can create that warm, cozy, enclosed effect as they bring the walls further *into* the space.

# PATTERN

Until recently, pattern has been seen as something of a naughty pleasure by many. All those serious interior designers who peddled schemes of unhindered minimalism and clean-surfaced restraint viewed the voluptuous delights of pattern with horror.

Like color, pattern comes with stories and associations that mean it always has a lot to say in a room. Large, full-blown floral patterns conjure up suggestions of traditional decorating and old-fashioned values. Imperialistic, abstract, organic patterns, such as damasks, can go either way—to some they mean history, royalty, and richness; to others they'll forever be associated with tacky flock wallpaper and over-decorated 1960s boudoirs. Stripes and plaids, by contrast, carry the gentlemanly whiff of old school tie, preppy rectitude, or failing that, Jane Austen primness.

As with selecting colors, choosing patterns will therefore always be personal, and personally, I like to research a pattern before committing to it. I like to know where it's from and how it was used so that I can really get under its skin. I find it helps when putting things together for a scheme to understand that a particular pattern has its roots in, say, Persian pattern-making tradition. With this in mind, I will then search out further elements from the same origin or with the same design inspiration. Then I will introduce it into the space where possible.

## Using pattern

*Repeat a pattern five times* From experience, I have always found very-small-scale, close-repeating patterns difficult to pull off in a design scheme. From a distance they tend to merge and become a bit of a mushy visual puddle. Be it wallpapers, blinds, or curtains, in an ideal world a good rule of thumb is to choose a pattern where a repeated motif can fit roughly five times vertically in the room. Any smaller, and I think you run the risk of busyness; any larger, and it will feel incomplete.

*More is often more* Just as a highly edited, minimalist room takes twice the budget, effort, and maintenance of an opulent scheme, so an outrageously joyful application of pattern on pattern provides more distraction and stimulation than a scheme conceived around one repeat. Putting patterns together takes a confident, decisive eye—not only do the colors need to be balanced, but there are motifs and repeats that also require consideration. Weirdly though, I find that the more patterns that are used within a space, the easier this is to pull off the desired effect.

*Apply to all four walls to maximize space* Pattern provides us with an important weapon in the war against small-scale space. Just as camouflage on a tank is there to confuse the eye and blur the outline, so the right sort of wallpaper (a paper with a strong contrast and non-geometric pattern) is the best room camouflage that money can buy. Over all four walls it does a brilliant vanishing act with the room's corners, while big, heavy bits of architecture like fireplaces, cumbersome cabinets, or clumsily placed doors can also be made to melt away in a haze of wallpaper pattern.

# LIGHTING

The relentless advance of technology has meant that something as simple as lighting a room has now become very complicated. As far as I am concerned, lighting in the home is simple if you remember the three golden rules: use lots of it, place it low, and illuminate up. Lighting the perimeter of a room is a good place to start; deliberately placing lamps in the corners of a room is a clever way of blurring its edges and increasing the overall sense of space. Likewise, placing lamps on low tables helps send light upwards, intensifying a feeling of a glowing enclosure and making the most of the room's vertical space. Whatever else you do, avoid using just one strong, centrally placed light source. Though this may work well in a morgue, it's a disaster in a domestic setting—casting highlights and shadows that will make everything and everyone look unbelievably ugly.

## CREATING A LIGHTING SCHEME

While having light where you need it is extremely important, working out where that lighting should go is always so much easier on paper. Drawing up a lighting scheme is a great opportunity to explore the different lighting possibilities that exist. The added result will be that a neat, finalized plan (if it results in the need for rewiring) can also be used by an electrician as a guide. Remember that, for large rooms and open-plan spaces in particular, it's important that a lighting scheme takes into account the whole area. There is no point in planning the lighting for the dining area of a living room, say, without considering the impact that this will have on the rest of the space, as it will just end up an incoherent mess.

Though it can be expensive, rewiring a room will mean that the power sources for your lighting will be exactly where they are needed. The result is not only more aesthetically pleasing and safer—as you won't need miles of ugly, dangerous extension cords in order to plug your light into the nearest wall outlet—it can also make life far more convenient. If I am having a room rewired, I will often opt for a plan that lets me switch on all the tall lamps from one point. So, no more having to jump up and down to switch off or on each lamp individually and no need to get out of bed to turn off all the lights in a room. What could be better?

## TYPES OF LIGHTING

While it's true that there are many flavors of light, as long as you can understand the differences between them you will be able to choose the light that is best suited to your space with confidence.

## INCANDESCENT BULBS

Most homes are lit by traditional incandescent bulbs that give a reliable, warm glow. Their effect can be varied by strength, as in wattage, or by an opaque pearlescent finish over the bulbs or even a color coating.

## HALOGEN BULBS

Down lights, spotlights, and many contemporary lamps use halogen. Low-voltage halogen gives off clean, pure light. As such it is used widely in stores to really show off a product to its best advantage. Its effect isn't a million miles away from daylight, so it is great in dark areas that have to be entirely artificially lit.

## COMPACT FLUORESCENT BULBS

Using compact fluorescent lightbulbs can be tricky. Depending upon where you live, however, they may be mandated by code. They save energy and provide plenty of illumination but little romance or subtlety. Energy-saving bulbs are best used inside strongly colored glass light fittings. If they are used in a conventional lamp base, I find a foil-lined lampshade in old gold or bronze to be the only way of counteracting their ugly, milky glow.

## FLUORESCENT BULBS

While being energy efficient, traditional fluorescent lighting has no subtlety whatsoever. Its strong, blue characteristic has a habit of sucking any warmth out of any interior it illuminates. The newer compact fluorescents mentioned above are better.

# *Using reflected light*

Loving nothing more than to boisterously bounce from shiny surfaces, reflected light helps in making a space feel lively and interesting. Furniture buffed to a highy polished sheen, light-reflecting silky or glazed fabrics, and lustrous foil wallpapers all do marvelous work at helping out daylight, while the following options can transform your room from dim to dazzling.

*Lay reflective flooring*   While wall-to-wall carpeting is a wonderful, voluptuous treat for the eyes and feet, it does gobble up daylight. Hard floor surfaces, such as wood, stone, or vinyl-resilient flooring, by contrast, reflect light magnificently. What few people realize, however, is that they do this job far better the darker they are.

*Choose leggy furniture*   There is no point in having all that light-reflecting potential on the floor if your room is choked up with heavy furniture—anything soft or absorbent will stop it dead in its tracks. Instead, go for leggy furniture, which will increase the sense of both light and space.

*Use art to light the way*   While not quite so obvious, I have often found that art can make a surprising difference to the light levels of a room. In very dark rooms, I'll often use pictures with deliberately over-generous pale ivory matting and narrow gold-leaf frames to help break up the gloom and act as regularly spaced light reflectors.

*Experiment with mirrors*   Mirrors reflect space, light, and shade, and used properly, can glam up any interior. For those who fear that their own reflection might prove to be (over time) too distracting, try placing a picture in front of the mirror at eye level. This means that the mirror does what it's there to do and reflects the room without constantly grabbing your attention. And don't see mirrors as just for walls. Pieces of mirror cut to size and used on specific bits of furniture can reflect light brilliantly.

# UTILITIES

For me there is no sense in denying the existence of twenty-first-century utilities and conveniences. Even in period interiors (in fact often especially in period interiors) I like to use technology in unashamedly head-on fashion. Indeed, provided they are properly and elegantly designed, there can often be a real design advantage gained by using a sprinkle of contemporary elements within a scheme.

## TV SCREENS

Since the advent of the flat screen, the TV is no longer the bullying, hulking presence it once was. I like to put TVs in busy contexts where there is a lot going on, so that the screen is not necessarily the first thing you see. On shelves or in bookcases, televisions become part of a much larger display and, as a result, are far less dominant. Their impact can also be lessened by integrating their black screens into a color scheme—perhaps by placing them next to a dark picture or a run of black-spined books. And if you do find their presence unbearably overwhelming, you can always try storing them in cabinets.

## ELECTRICAL OUTLETS AND SWITCHES

Now that electrical outlets and switches come in designed finishes, such as slate, copper, glass, chrome, or brass, I like to see them as accents—with their position on a wall and their relationship with all other elements within the room carefully considered. Where wallpaper is the hero of the scheme, subtle acrylic paneled switches that let the paper show through have a lot going for them, for example.

## RADIATORS

If you live in an older home or apartment, you may have radiators. Provided they have been properly integrated into a scheme and their inclusion has been thoroughly thought through, I really do not object to seeing radiators in a home. Putting a shelf over a radiator is an idea that I am very keen on. From a practical perspective, this helps to redirect heat efficiently back into the room as well as reducing heat damage to the wall, while aesthetically it creates an opportunity for displaying eye-catching "still lives" that can distract attention away from the radiator below. If, however, you do want to minimize a radiator's visual impact, try either painting it to blend in with a wall or render it invisible by placing it behind an open-back bookcase or sofa, from where it will function perfectly happily. However, don't block the heat.

# Storage

While there are going to be some things in life that don't get used everyday, to be honest I find myself at a loss when faced with the current obsession with "storage." It is all part and parcel of minimalism, I suppose—though any minimalist statement fails dismally if, rather than reducing your life to an essential essence, it merely sweeps it under the carpet. My general feeling is that if you have got stuff that cannot be put on display, then why have it in the first place?

*Store in plain sight*  I admit I am a maximalist. I love to be surrounded by objects I own that give me pleasure. I love the combinations and relationships they strike up, and I love being able to relive the experiences that accompany them. Generally speaking, then, wherever I can I like to use chunky open shelves on which books, lamps, plants, and clutter all jostle for good-natured attention.

*Integrate storage into your design scheme*
Of course, not everything you own can be out on display. Even I would balk at a shelf displaying an inflatable dinghy, Christmas ornaments, and a toolbox. So a degree of storage will always be necessary. Where you do need it, try to incorporate it into your design scheme as early as possible. If conceived at an early stage in the development of your room, cabinets, baskets, bins, and boxes can work within the architectural layout of a space and provide you with all the practical storage solutions you need, while remaining neat and discreet.

# ROOMS TO INSPIRE

WALLPAPER CUT TO SHAPE

BED SIDE ON

PUN

EGALITE

WARDROBE DOORS

TV

PARENTAL RETREAT

Baroque 'n' roll

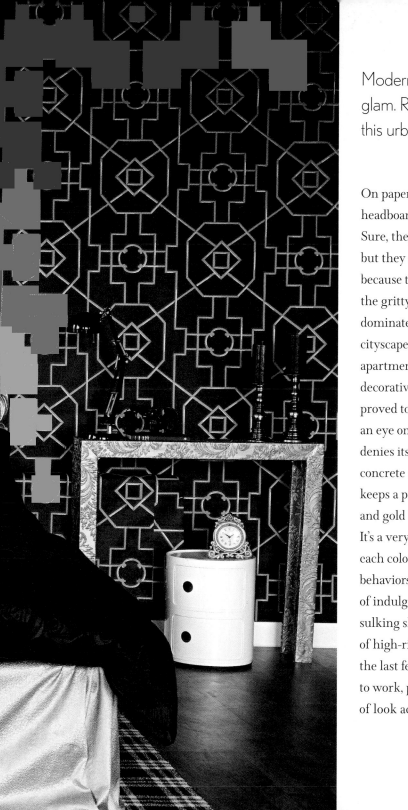

Modern design doesn't have to hold back on the glam. Riding the revival of interest in all things rich, this urban pad blings very brightly indeed.

On paper the tartan carpet, the gold trellis paper, the ornate headboard, and a wall of postcards shouldn't really work. Sure, they are bits and pieces from many different sources, but they all sit more than happily in the same scheme because they are all based on grid patterns. I was inspired by the gritty urban detailing of the gridded balcony fronts that dominate the foreground of the formerly industrialized cityscape beyond the window of this modern urban apartment. I loved the idea of taking something so anti-decorative and using it as a starting point for what has proved to be an indulgent visual feast. But all along I've kept an eye on context, and there's nothing about this space that denies its contemporary architectural style. Even the bare concrete ceiling has a part to play in ensuring that this room keeps a particularly rock-and-roll flavored edge to it. Black and gold has always been a high-calorie color combination. It's a very naughty story, and one that relies on the fact that each color brings out quite the most attention-grabbing behaviors in the other. Against black, gold becomes a beacon of indulgence, and on gold, black is transformed into a dense, sulking shadow. This scheme is a perfect example of the sort of high-risk, high-return decorating I love. It was only when the last few elements arrived that the room suddenly started to work, proving how finely balanced the success of this sort of look actually is.

1

# Art attack

This ever-changing wall of postcards from an art gallery is a wonderful way of furnishing a workstation. Images can be added or subtracted depending on inspiration. I grudgingly suppose that lists, timetables, schedules, or takeout menus could be included—if needed. The console tables were made very simply from medium-density fiberboard (MDF) that was covered in Anaglypta, a very old-fashioned, heavy paper. Its rich, undulating patterns look surprisingly modern on a clean-lined piece of furniture like this—particularly when gold leafed.

## Leaving camp behind

Although there's plenty of opulence here, it's really only the eye-catching headboard that undulates with historical largesse. Everything else is kept elegant with a highly contemporary sense of sleek, clean-lined chic.

## On reflection

Like Alice's door through to Lookingglassford-shire, the large, ornately framed mirror propped in the corner (below) bounces light around the room, helping to open up the space.

## Golden oldie

This fabulous floor cushion sums up what is for me a real high-octane, high-impact scheme. It's the kinky combination of gilt leather and slouched comfort that never fails to raise a wry smile. Yes, it's all a bit unapologetically nightclubby, but at least it's the VIP area.

◆ Painting a wall 148 ◆ Applying wallpaper 168-9 ◆ Laying laminate flooring 202 ◆ Gold leafing 227 ◆

The wonder of one

There was a time when one-room living carried all sorts of sad baggage with it—the "studio apartment" was a place that came complete with broken dreams and string vests. No longer. Today the one-room space has undergone a dramatic transformation into the fabulously glamorous *pied à terre*.

Strictly speaking, this wonderful warehouse conversion is five stories away from the *terre* so I suppose it is actually a *pied à ciel*. Whatever you call it, there's a lot of chunky architectural detail in this apartment that has survived the gentrification process from warehouse to swanky loft. All that hewn block and oak beam come with a strong flavor, so I settled on a mouth-watering color scheme that can live happily alongside the industrial architectural leftovers. Yellow is never an easy color in a northern climate. With gray skies and greenish light reflected from all that lush countryside, it can end up terribly acidic. Here, carefully applied blocks of color bring a sunny warmth to the gray architectural details, while yellow's dominant personality is contained and tamed by its white surroundings. The layout of the apartment, defined by the original architecture, is long and narrow with more than a hint of the corridor to it. So big, brash, bold blocks of color designate zones and create a sense of arrival. All the tricks of the trade have been used here to make sure that light is maximized. Furniture has been lifted off the floor on shiny legs and light-reflecting surfaces abound, while a sunlight-intensifying, darkly glossy wooden floor makes the space feel open, light, and bright.

2

# Here comes the sun

In this room, light is of paramount importance. Even the display shelves have been conceived so that they won't block precious light or cast gloomy shadows. And the rich, yellow color block creates an eye-catching feature for the middle of the wall. Sprinkled yellowy greens and the odd lime accent calms down the potentially tricky yellow, making it feel more natural and less acidic.

Despite being up in the sky, this apartment does suffer from a lack of privacy from nearby neighbors. Because light is at a premium in this space, I designed this laser-cut screen as a portable, contemporary take on the semi-sheer curtain. The screen blocks the specific problem area, leaving the rest of the window to flood light into the room.

## Sun-kissed sunflowers

These self-adhering wall stickers of William Morris-inspired sunflowers gave me an excellent opportunity to bring a bit of pattern and interest to the walls without cluttering them. Having just the odd motif means the eye-catching texture of the exposed block wall does not have to compete with the adjacent pattern.

## On the level

As a way of grappling with the long, narrow layout, the kitchen sits on a raised platform covered with slate tiles (above right). This change in height and difference in materials peps up what might otherwise be a rather one-note space. It also provides concealment for utilities, such as gas, water, and electricity through to the long, narrow working unit and creates a boundary between kitchen and corridor.

## Shiny happy people

The modern furniture in glossy plastic and light-reflecting lacquer gives this scheme what the previous generation would refer to as "space age chic"...rather funny, really. But this classic retro-inspired look in the context of the all-white kitchen does have a kind of star-ship charm along with an ability to bounce back those rays.

All-natural ingredients

Here, a basement kitchen proves that beige needn't be boring if texture is used to bring a bit of touchy-feely sensuality to a scheme.

When you think about it, nature is never dull. Everywhere you look, light and shadow bring life to every surface. Naturally rough, smooth, shiny, or matte surfaces create a constantly scintillating palette of contrasts. In this kitchen, somewhat cursed by an urban basement view, I used Mother Nature as a muse and sought out eye-pleasing pieces that possess an often wry relationship with natural objects. Vases that look like blades of grass, bowls that look like broad leaves, and a candlestick that could almost fool a cactus spotter all help to bring a healthy outdoor breeze into a downstairs world that could have otherwise felt like a sunless, subterranean burrow. A neutral, earthy color scheme has been used here to continue the natural theme. Decorating like this is notoriously difficult. Naturals, neutrals, beiges, taupes, or "greiges" (gray-ish beiges) all have their own color top note—what looks like a completely colorless linen can be quite unapologetically green if put next to a beige that errs toward pink, for example. Thankfully, here the neutrals all have a close kinship with yellow and green, which ensures that they all get on well together.

# $\mathcal{B}$eware beige blindness

Natural or neutral tones respect tough-love decorating, so don't fear strong emphatic contrasts. The black/brown tiling behind the range and the dark, shiny slate used for the work surfaces both help to nudge the paler shades into the far distance. They've been used to deliberately command attention and take the eye to the focal point created by the range. Likewise an artificial-turf-like rug breaks up the wood laminate floor and brings some color (and a little of the outdoors) into the room. The use of contrast in this space is essential; without it, the room would slackly unravel into an amorphous beige blob.

## Cutting corners

Fitting a kitchen requires a lot of thought. In this case, there was only one place for the range—where the fireplace used to be. A fireplace is rarely deep enough to fit a modern appliance. For a nice, neat and consistent line, I had the face of the fireplace brought forward to create a generous surround (opposite). This frames the range as well as giving a neat, upright to finish the storage units on either side.

## Sitting pretty

I love kitchens that feel like sitting rooms. We now spend so much time in them, why shouldn't we furnish our kitchens with something a little more comfortable to sit on than simple kitchen chairs? Here, a generously upholstered banquette (below) brings a note of soft comfort to the space. As the banquette is built around a radiator with a grill on top, its real gift is most apparent in winter, when it becomes a a fabulously heated seat.

## Cool drawers

In unashamedly naked metal, refrigerator drawers (below left) have been conceived to fit in with the kitchen cabinets. This does away with the need for a tall, visually obstructive model and allows for uninterrupted runs of the slate countertop providing the neat, sleek, tailored look that fits this kitchen's scheme.

◆ Painting a wall 148 ◆ Painting woodwork 196 ◆ Hanging a mirror 196 ◆ Laying laminate flooring 202 ◆

Bath night at the opera

This is for everyone who feels that, come bath time, they want to be a diva with a loofah, a Carmen in a shower cap, or a Brunhilde in a tub of bubbles.

Think of the great icons of femininity, and the odds are that you'll think of them in the bath (well, at least I always find I do). Cleopatra, Messalina, Lucrezia Borgia, Lady Hamilton, Marilyn Monroe—they all conjure sensual images of indulgent bath times. From the quivering slicks of twinkling bubbles to the rare, exotic unguents in voluptuous-looking vessels, the truly glamorous know that nothing suits them better than a tub and nothing else. Here, I've quite shamelessly exploited the theatrical potential to be wrung from a freestanding red-lacquered bathtub in an all-black bathroom. Patterns undulate in feminine whiplashes, while straight lines are kept to a well-edited minimum so that the entire environment works hard to celebrate the decorative potential of womanly curves. This is an unapologetic fantasy room—a highly contrived cocoon in which to escape the gray, grim reality of twenty-first century living. And why not? The very act of bathing is to immerse oneself into a warm, scented comfort zone as an antidote, an escape, a recharge. The difference here is that the the bathroom *looks* as sensually indulgent as bath time always feels.

# Beauty from within

Unfortunately the cluttered-up reality of bathing is a thousand and one ugly bottles containing everything from shampoo to contact-lens solution. In this bathroom, panels pop open to reveal the purple interiors of generous cabinets (opposite top right) that can be called upon to discreetly but conveniently contain such unattractive necessities.

## Shower curtain call

Because the bathroom opens straight from the next-door dressing room, the heavy-paneled architecture that visually divides the two immediately feels like the proscenium arch of a theater. The fact that the bathroom steps up causes people to assume I've created a stage to match. In fact, the raised floor is purely practical, accommodating the plumbing as well as the very necessary support beams that were installed to stop the heavy bath (made heavier when full of water) from crashing through to the floor below.

## Down the line

Just about the only straight lines in this bathroom decorate the black-lacquer paneling (opposite right). Providing a light-reflecting touch of opulence, they were very easily created with the help of a gold marker pen and ruler. Perhaps more than anything else, it's the luxurious twinkles of gold that make this bathroom look like a box at the opera.

◆ Painting woodwork  150  ◆ Hanging a mirror 196  ◆ "Gold leaf" lining 230  ◆ Covering a lampshade with wallpaper 234 ◆

## Reflected glory

An alcove lined with black mirror contains a bulbous modern basin of my design and an ultra-contemporary faucet. I had the mirror drilled so that I could hang an antique framed Venetian mirror on top for a clearer reflection. Because the bathroom is open to the rest of the master suite, both the toilet and the basin have been tucked away to the sides of the room. This ensures they remain out of sight in the wings, leaving the red-lacquer diva bath very much center stage.

## Hiding the tank

The modern toilet I designed for this bathroom features a tank that has been concealed behind a panel. By bringing the wall forward far enough to conceal this, I was also able to create yet more storage behind it in the shape of another purple-lacquered cabinet. I loved the idea of including a sudden and unapologetic splurge of modernity like this within such a theatrical scheme.

Living in the closet

These days, bachelors have high standards when it comes to their pads. Discarded pizza boxes and sweaty sport socks are most definitely not the look *du jour*. Instead, boy boudoirs should have a sophisticated cosmopolitan air to them that betrays an understandable interest in the pulling power of a posh *pied à terre*.

This highly convenient apartment occupies a relatively small footprint. So, like a Swiss Army penknife, rooms fold away when not in use. The sleeping area is easily separated from the living and cooking quarters by giant, fuchsia-lacquered folding screens. For this scheme, I wanted to bring a restrained sprinkling of pattern and interest to the walls without cluttering. So I took inspiration from sportswear and painted what I suppose could only be described as "go faster" stripes over the bed. Aesthetically, they help, with a minimum of fuss and bother, to unify a space that could have felt disjointed. Casually casting around for something to bring interest, I hit upon the idea of heraldry. The clubby connotations of coats of arms also provide considerable design potential in this simple stripped-back scheme. The shields on the walls were created with stencils and pick up the brown, silver, and red color scheme as well as forging a preppy relationship with the gorgeous heirloom antique drums casually used as tables. This is a room where there's just about the right amount going on. It's not actually minimal, but neither is it a fruit salad buffet of high-maintenance clutter. The perfect compromise for today's metropolitan, urbane neo-dandy.

5

# Seeing stripes

Using low-tack masking tape, a straightedge, and latex paint, I created these stripes as a more or less instantaneous way of bringing emphasis to a room. The thick bands and thinner lines impart a decidedly retro 80s feel that sits well in this loft-like context. On-the-diagonal stripes create maximum impact with minimum means, leaving enough bare wall around them to keep the feel of the room open and spacious.

## Human shield

The coffee tabletop, with its magnificent coat of arms, is in fact a large digital print under glass (bottom left). Heraldry has a graphic richness that balances detail with crisp, clean lines. It is, I reckon, the ultimate in boy badges. The linen cushions on the sofas were also very simply made using graphic, heraldry-inspired blocks of fabric appliquéd onto store-bought pillow covers.

## History lesson

In uncompromisingly modern spaces, I always like to insert an object or two that doesn't rhyme with contemporary taste and that has a romance or history that takes it far beyond the here and now. I loved these wonderful drums (opposite; right; bottom center) on sight and knew they'd be a perfect point of interest in this urban yet urbane scheme. There aren't many opportunities for embellishment and pattern in the boy zone, so plundering military history like this is an effective way of injecting a bit of guy glamor into this room.

◆ Painting stripes 159 ◆ Stencilling 164 ◆ Making your own wallpaper with laser transfers 176 ◆ Laying laminate flooring 202 ◆

Contemporary cocoon

Time was, the countryside was seen as a backwater. Taste, it was thought, ended at the first sighting of open space, while style, if it existed at all in the country, was shabby but never chic.

But all that's changed. There now exists a new breed of rural retreaters who expect their country environment to come with as much style as a hip hotel in the city. Here among the rural idyll, a tumbledown old stone building has been reincarnated as an uber-chic chill-out zone. The textures and particular details of the agricultural vernacular typical of the area are left to speak for themselves. But by using the soft, cool, tailored furniture you'd typically expect to see in a modern metropolitan loft, the mellow history of the stone walls and the oak beams become heightened by contrast. There's an erogenous commitment to ensuring that this place can be enjoyed as a comfort zone. Sofas as big as beds frame an enormous contemporary fireplace set into the old stone walls, while the lighting is kept low key and sexily amber colored to ensure that the mood remains lusciously laid back. The only note of energy in this space are the cavorting sculptures that have been dotted around to cast deliberately abstract, excitingly curvaceous shadows in the warm, glowing half light.

6

# Country decorating gets hip

It's a real country-house classic—a pair of comfortable sofas placed at right angles to a generous fire. Snuggled as close as possible to the warmth of the flames, it's the perfect arrangement for conversation, relaxation, or post-Sunday-dinner coma. The breezy width of circulation space behind each sofa ensures that the attention is focused firmly on the center of the room.

## Light-fingered lighting

Getting the lighting right makes a room. Here, the rich, orange glow of the fire has inspired lighting choices that work hard not to shatter the seductive atmosphere. Amber glass globes resonate a rich, warm light, while up lights installed in the floor caress the texture of the walls. There's nothing harsh, nothing overhead, nothing to break the spell. To be honest, locating a lost contact lens takes forever in this glamorous gloom, but that's always going to be a problem in chill-out zones such as this one.

◆ *Cleaning a surface for painting 146* ◆ *Painting a wall 149* ◆ *"Aging" new floorboards 206* ◆

## Refined dining

At the other end of the room, a light well creates a bright, elegant dining area to contrast with the adjacent snug, fire-lit atmosphere. By using this kind of twentieth-century thoroughbred furniture, the dining area feels like a metropolitan oasis of sleek chic, which only serves to make the mothering warmth of the fire feel that much more compelling.

## Techno-deco

Stadium-concert-quality surround sound and movie-premiere-level home cinema have been tactfully integrated in this high-tech yet Old World space. A lattice of beams on the ceiling conceal wiring and speakers, while the great techno engine room that runs the show is discreetly veiled by a hand-forged contemporary screen. On a windowsill, there's a vintage-style radio (above left). It's an oddly piquant statement of retro over techno: the radio we love to see, all those matte-black woofers and graphic equalizers we'd rather hide.

NEWT

ELVE

$\mathcal{B}$usy bathroom

This family bathroom has to change from being a busy, efficient machine for scrubbing and brushing in the morning into a sensual, watery retreat for a hardworking mom (or dad) at bath time.

While being light, bright, and convenient are all any of us need from a bathroom during the morning scramble when the emphasis is on getting ready and getting out, we'd all prefer something more inviting for an evening bath-time treat. Part of the problem is all that white. The bath, the basin, the toilet, the tiles—if you're not careful, a typical bathroom can give you snow blindness. Here, I've used a sleek, elegant gray that reflects daylight when needed but also looks wonderfully sophisticated in the evening. It doesn't compromise the clean, modern feel of the space, but it does knock the edge off the overlit operating-theater atmosphere from which white bathrooms suffer at night. It's also the perfect foil for the citrus-rich orange shades I wanted to include to invigorate the family's eyes in the morning. Because part of my goal was to persuade the children to be a little tidier, I commissioned a charming hand-drawn mural that shows them how to do it, illustrating clutter neatly put away on shelves. Throughout the mural there are loads of family references and in-jokes to keep a smile on everyone's face, while all the family are encouraged to help themselves to the pot of white marker pens and add to the artwork for a really personal touch. The result is a family-centric bathroom space that is flexible enough to accommodate four very different personalities.

7

# Bath-time banter

To really get mom in the mood for a fabulously indulgent evening soak, there's a sketched bottle of wine at the ready and a prettily drawn decorative table on which to put a bath-time chocolate bar. It's in-jokes and witty references such as these that can make a scheme fun for the whole family. Remember, if at any time the joke falls flat, you can always paint out the offending item.

## Oodles of doodles

The inevitable storage solutions we all take for granted in bathrooms have here been incorporated into the giant doodle. Cabinets and shelves exist as drawings as well as real elements. Drawing the clutter in a room is an amusing way of encouraging the younger bathroom inhabitants to keep the real, less-attractive clutter under control, providing a specific example of how and where things, such as towels and toothbrushes, should be stored.

## In the frame

An over-grand frame brings a note of graphic glamour to what is otherwise a very ordinary mirror. Because the markers are always on hand and can be so easily covered with paint, there's nothing to stop shopping lists, homework diaries, timetables, or aide-mémoire notes from finding their way onto the walls.

## Fun to store

Buckets sprayed in shiny orange enamel have been painted with the children's names to encourage them to look after and take responsibility for their own bath-time clutter. This is a great way of sorting out differences of opinion as to ownership (shall we say) and helps to get them used to putting things away.

◆ Painting a wall 149 ◆ Tiling 180 ◆ Hanging a mirror 196 ◆ Laying laminate flooring 202 ◆ Installing a roller blind 222 ◆

Like a lot of spaces that have been converted into apartments from old warehouses, this one's beaming from eave to eave. However, the danger of this vogue for letting it all hang out when it comes to structural elements is that it can often lead to rooms that fall short of cozy.

When I first saw this room, it was a case of contrast taking a step too close to the edge of edgy—a complex cat's cradle of dark beams set against Hollywood-smile white plaster. To jump the gap between beam and wall (and to bring in the sloped ceiling for a warming goodnight cuddle), I painted over the brilliant white with a rich shade of wine red. My design inspiration for this room was the oaky barrel flavor of the rich wood used to panel in the headboard. Oh, and the fact that this former wine warehouse still seemed to ooze delicious hints of rich, red alcohol. Perhaps I was imagining it. Perhaps it was just thirst, but the final scheme has a scrumptiously strong taste to it with colors that have been chosen to hold eye, nose, and throat in flavorful awe. It's a good illustration of how shades from the same chromatic vineyard can be used to bring rich depths and fruity top notes to a scheme. Notice the blueberry-purple pillow among all those rich sweet shades of red, a tart accent that surprises and uplifts the room. Finally, glowing in the shadows, a collection of copper objects, despite their more traditional kitchen associations, work extremely well in this masculine bedroom.

8

*A* bon viveur bedroom

# Handy headboard

The rich paneled box used as a headboard disguises all sorts of structural bits. Suffice it to say that, thanks to the attic-like geometry of the slanting roof, the headboard is able to accommodate pocket shelves built into either end (opposite top left). They are useful for storing bedtime books, the TV remote, and the like. Meanwhile, the top of the headboard makes for a great place to create an ever-changing still-life display. A dramatis personae of objects awaiting a walk-on part include a variety of copper vessels, a wonderful Arts and Crafts bowl, and an antique pastry cutter, while a collection of framed drawings from the Arts and Crafts era create the backdrop for the still-lifers.

◆ *Painting a wall* 149 ◆ *Making your own wallpaper with laser transfers* 176 ◆ *Hanging a picture* 196 ◆

## Best cellar

Wine labels are designed to look thirst-makingly delicious, and during *la belle époque* (the end of the nineteenth century) they flourished. In order to bring a little of that historical glamour to this bedroom, I scanned some of my favorite labels before printing them onto laser transfer paper to turn them into instant wall transfers. When placing these on the walls, I went for balance rather than symmetry, ensuring that the density of motifs wasn't any greater in one place than another. Notice the pillow on the bed. Here, a personalized toile du Juoy pattern has been created by printing a motif onto laser transfer paper. It has been attached to the dough-colored glazed chintz of the pillow fabric by ironing the image on the reverse side.

## Rougie bougie

Nestled in the dormer, a pair of Edwardian corner chairs make an elegant place from which to check out the view of the docks below. The ruby luster of the red lamp base looks just as good when the sun is out and the bulb is unlit as it does when lighting up the room at night.

# Retro retrod

There are those who find the deliberate revival of the styles of our childhood rather worrying. But why not fill a family comfort zone with references to happier days?

This magnificent kitchen living space expresses the ultimate in contemporary architectural chic. It ticks off an impressive number of the boxes that appear on today's style wish list—lots of light, acres of space, and loads of glass—as well as coming complete with some excitingly understated detailing. The tendency for rooms like this to lack soul has been countered here with a bravura attitude to decorating. Wallpaper inspired by the geometric patterns of the late '60s helps to bring the longest wall forward in a friendly, familiar embrace, while vintage accessories, as well as contemporary elements with a retro spin, help to give the room a sophisticated sense of lived-in fashionability. Finally, a relaxed attitude to the pillows and fabrics used on the seating unit helps to underline the fact that this room has to be both an affable family space *and* a high-end design statement. There is a temptation to underdecorate and underfurnish contemporary rooms such as this, ultimately creating a somewhat sterile space. By allowing some controlled clutter, this slick scheme succeeds in being high design but not high maintenance.

9

# Why retro is better than vintage

Retro (as in designed to look old) will always have the edge on vintage, the real stuff from the period. Here, this luxurious kitchen in striped wood veneer and stone goes so much further and is so much more convenient than the late 1960s kitchen that inspired it. It's like looking back at the fashion magazines of the past. Sure, I'm often struck by how nice the clothes are, but it's always painfully obvious that what fashion needed most was the invention of conditioner. Fly-away hair? Never.

## Pattern on pattern

An extremely relaxed attitude to mixing patterns helps to give this room a marvelously informal feeling. The table runner carries all the colors of the wallpaper, but its stylized, natural curves—which take inspiration from the modernist designers of the Art Deco period who influenced the geo-chic patterns of the '60s—couldn't be further from the paper's rectilinear forms.

## Glass act

The oak stairway up to the hallway boasts a seamless glass balustrade (Can you find it?) that gives an uninterrupted sense of space throughout the area. Glass has been cleverly used here so as not to compromise the light levels of such a long, narrow room. It creates enclosure without visually constraining the space.

## Let's hear it for the design

People often forget that design can be heard as well as seen. Ultra-contemporary interiors with lots of hard shiny surfaces create chilly, uncomfortable acoustics that can be at odds with relaxed family living. Bundles of cushions, shaggy shag rugs, big linen lamp shades—even canvasses on the wall—all help to absorb sound and create a space that is more conducive to chatter and children.

What happens when you find yourself sharing your hallway with historic wallpaper? Do you live with it? Live up to it? Or can you somehow make it work?

The temptation here was to either start again and hide all those twittering birds behind something more contemporary, or (worse still) do a Victorian version of "Pimp my Hall" and make this space into a travesty of nineteenth-century taste. My solution was to suggest that this young couple shy away from compromise and confront the historicized atmosphere with ultra-contemporary furniture. The result is a space that relies on a strong sense of improbability for its success. The simple geometry of the modern ice white pieces becomes coolly refreshing. Their crisp simplicity acts as antidote to the aviary context of the undulating 1870s paper. Like a starched white shirt brought up to date by a richly patterned tie, this elegant, highly fashionable scheme revels in the incongruity of space-age furniture in a costume-drama context.

(10)

# Making an entrance

## Hanging hint

When you are hanging pictures in a hallway, bear in mind that they will be viewed at an ever-changing eye level. As you go up a staircase, hanging a group of pictures in an ascending block increases the sense of height as well as giving you something diverting to look at on the way to bed (below and opposite left).

# *The* call of the hall

Never forget that, unlike rooms where we spend time, hallways have an audience constantly on the move. They're transitional spaces that don't have one particularly dominant viewpoint or axis. Keep hallway design on the hoof with points of interest to brighten what is an ever-changing interior vista as you move around the space. As you don't spend a lot of time in them, hallways and staircases can profit from a big-brush-stroke attitude to interior design. Try treating them to schemes where your normal design comfort zone has been expanded or where the color knob gets turned up a bit. They'll love you for it.

◆ *Painting woodwork 150* ◆ *Applying wallpaper 168–9* ◆ *Hanging a picture 196* ◆ *"Aging" new floorboards 206* ◆

## Past and present: a very modern marriage

I've always believed that the past would be extremely surprised to find itself treated with the awed respect we show it today. Back in the 1870s, when this wallpaper was created, design legacy was being constantly brought up to date as new styles came into fashion. These days, we're either one thing or another—ultracontemporary or fundamentally traditional. This hall proves that by making room for both in the same space, chic can be elegantly achieved .

## Wainscot

Halls need to be practical. They get a real hammering from people straight from the wet or muddy great outdoors. Wainscot is macho enough to cope with most things and was invented to provide a practical paneled finish for rough-and-tumble rooms, such as hallways. Cover it using a washable latex paint. Any bumps or marks can be quickly and easily touched up—which is as easy as maintenance gets.

# $\mathscr{A}$ secret lair with flair

Why is it that the devil gets all the best tunes and villains get all the best pads? While no one remembers what James Bond's place looked like, Dr. No, Goldfinger, Blofeld, et al., have left us with a lasting impression of *grande luxe* interiors found inside some of the most surprising secret lairs.

This part conversion (from a windmill), part new build is the perfect background for some opulent, villain-inspired decorating. The temptation with a space like this is to try to match the modernity of the architecture to furniture and furnishings that show far too many bolts. So-called modern design "classics" (more deserving of the term clichés) would have made this open-plan living room irritatingly predictable. Instead, French nineteenth-century furniture—with its frivolous gilding and poison green damask upholstery—has been used to luxe up this lounge and force the envelope we've marked "good taste" to be opened and its contents reexamined. This scheme is not, however, as simplistic as old furniture, new house. Modern pieces feature heavily, but they have been chosen principally for their well-tailored discretion. Like perfectly conceived contemporary display cases in a modern museum of Victorian taste, the sleekly simplistic sofa, ottoman, dining table, and chairs in this space all offer the perfect perch for the display of ornate opulence that brings this room alive.

11

# Home cinema

This room unabashedly takes its interior inspiration from film, and why not? Some of the most iconic design moments have been entirely motivated by the medium. The golden age of Bond gave the world some astonishing interiors, and it was the decadent modernism of the villain's lair that has remained one of my evergreen aesthetic inspirations. With taste as good as his character was bad, the classic Bond villain surrounded himself with the exquisite, the recherché, and the obviously recently stolen. It's touches such as the gilded green-damask-upholstered wooden chair—which, like a time traveler, has somehow found its way into this twenty-first-century underground eco-home from a Parisian salon in the 1890s—that capture this feeling and help to make this space so energetically sexy.

◆ Painting a wall 149 ◆ Hanging a mirror 196 ◆ Tiling 180 ◆ Covering a lampshade with wallpaper 234 ◆

## Cabinet of curiosities

Deliberately using things in a room scheme because they're interesting rather than pretty or indeed the height of fashion really floats my boat. For the Georgians, a cabinet full of often quirky, sometimes costly, but always extraordinary objects was their answer to TV—the minerals, fossils, and taxidermically preserved marvels had to capture the attention and fill the long nights. This glass-fronted shop cabinet filled with stalactites is a blast from the Georgian past.

## Socket and see

Strangely, the thing that gives me the most pleasure about the image below isn't the fabulously sexy cast-acrylic standard lamp in the shape of a Baroque candlestick; it's not the elegant Louis *quell-que-chose* console table; it's not even the green damask chair—it's the outlets and receptacles. In case you hadn't noticed, this is the twenty-first century, and we need to be able to accommodate power outlets, telephone connections, and cables. Fine as far as I'm concerned, but let's make them part of the design from the outset. Here, a West Point cadet lineup of electrical possibilities is waiting for the great switch-on.

## Table manners

A sleek, contemporary glass dining table comes alive with a decadent Baroque tablescape of gold, gold, and, well, more gold. Obviously one's knee-jerk reaction in this space would be to set the table with dignified modernist cutlery in shades of Scandinavian. But there's no word for feast in the dictionary of minimalism, so why not raise the ghost of dinner parties past and give this modernist placement the opulent makeover it deserves?

Ultra violet

For this mid-nineteenth-century townhouse, I was asked to create a scheme that would celebrate the room's impressive proportions, make an elegant background to entertaining, and have wow factors by the spade-full.

Rooms such as this are made for wallpaper. The Victorian era, when this house was built, was the great heyday of pattern. I've always found that just painting walls in rooms this size often leaves them feeling flat and uninhabited. The unusual decision for violet came from out of the ether, yet I knew that to balance such a decadent color the room would need a sophisticated application of slate gray. This wallpaper is one of my own designs, and I'm extremely fond of it. While the scale of the repeat works just as well in spaces with high or low ceilings, it's the colors—the twinkle of cool gold and gloss black—that make such an elegant statement. As is often the case with houses of this age, the deep alcoves on either side of the fireplace don't quite match. Papered to match the walls, the chunky shelves help to rebalance this anomaly and provide a stage upon which theatrical groupings of carefully chosen objects can be choreographed. I'm immensely fond of papering shelves or bookcases. It's an instant, easy, and hugely economical way of finishing inexpensive wood shelving that looks great. These days veneering shelves in rich showy woods is exceedingly expensive, while simply painting them, I think, just doesn't look right. This is the sort of project I relish, where a contemporary sensibility has to be elegantly fused with a room's historical proportions.

12

# Balancing act

Symmetry works hard to promote a sense of dependable decorum and pleasure in any room. Here, Victorian furniture is given a restrained makeover with purple suede, black velvet, and slinky satin. Although the furniture in this room doesn't always exactly match itself on either side of a center line, I've worked hard to give the space a feeling of balance. Thanks to the street-facing windows, this ground-floor room can suffer from a lack of privacy when the shutters are opened. Instead of resorting to curtains, a lush window box of lavender helps to partially obscure the view from outside in, while still allowing plenty of light into the room.

◆ *Painting a wall 149* ◆ *Applying wallpaper 168–69* ◆ *Covering a shelf with wallpaper 172* ◆ *Gold leafing 227* ◆ *Faking white gold leaf 227* ◆

## By prior arrangement

While symmetry may not always be possible, balance is. Compositions of objects work when the visual weight of one side is balanced on the other. On this cabinet (right), visual equilibrium has been achieved by balancing the large lamp and shade with a collection of photo frames.

## Sense of proportion

This room has a heavily ornate cornice (above) typical of its period. To lighten the visual load and to make the room feel even taller, I painted half of it the same shade as the wallpaper. This visually pushes the ceiling up, making it seem further away.

## All that glitters

Clusters of reflective, twinkling objects continue the theme of metallic luxury started by the wallpaper. Silver baubles and frames adorn a variety of surfaces, while a shamelessly opulent handful of different shades of gold bring life to the marble mantelpiece (far left). There are few decorating projects more satisfying than working with gold leaf. Though it obviously doesn't come cheap, it will make a dramatic impact in any room—even when used in small quantities. And if you long for the luster of all things gold and glittery but don't quite have the budget for the real thing, fear not—it can be effectively (and affordably) faked.

All too often, a three-quarter bath is space stolen from another room...and it looks it. However, a built-in or freestanding shower has become something of a contemporary necessity. But there's no reason why the space—sometimes one of the smallest rooms in the house—shouldn't have the biggest impact.

Like a lot of these rooms, this space was really just a collection of fixtures before I got my hands on it. With no windows, no architectural details, and no personality, it made for a perfectly blank canvas onto which I painted an evocative interior inspired by *grande luxe* travel, opulent finishes, and Art Deco glamour. Budget forbade expensive marble panels on the walls and the light-reflective marble floor I might have used, so instead marbled wallpaper with glistening foil veining was cut into squares and then stuck onto the wall in an alternating checkerboard of *eau de nil* and ebony. This is a classically exotic Art Deco color combination inspired by the waters of the River Nile and the fabulously recherché brown/black of African hardwood. The diagonal lattice theme also makes it onto the vinyl-tile floor. Though the look may be retro, there's a lot of very up-to-date elements in this space. Radiant floor heating (which works extremely well under vinyl tiles) warms the room, while an electronic sensor-controlled faucet provides carefully calculated hot water at the approach of a hand—doing away with the visual clutter of taps. The chilly expanse of glass that we're so used to seeing in showers has been turned into an Art Deco screen inspired by one I'd seen on the Orient Express. But rather than budget-busting Lalique, this is a vinyl transfer made from my design by a local sign company.

13

# Hero of the shower

# Trompe l'eau

Visual tricks aplenty have been used to give this tiny shower room character and a greater sense of space. On either side of the door, with its digital print panel of Venice at high water, a pair of highly convenient cabinets hold towels and other necessities. Black-painted base trim is easily mistaken for additional floor space, while the checkerboard papers camouflage and distract the perspective of this full-but-tailored space.

## Cool metal

Believe it or not, faucets can clash. While bathroom fittings might all look like the same color, they'll often be slightly different shades of chrome, bronze, or another metal. Here, shades of nickel and white-gold leaf exist happily alongside the chrome highlights of this modern bathroom, knitting everything together. Mini crystal chandeliers hang glamorously over otherwise unremarkable halogen down lights. The faceted droplets cast shards of rainbow across the silvery reflective surfaces of the shower room and heighten the feeling of being in a *grande luxe* cabin, bound for somewhere glamorously foreign.

## A touch of glass

The turquoise glass handle is the only hint that a cabinet is lurking behind the marble wallpaper. Building storage on either side of a centrally placed door creates a small lobby space. When cabinets are given an identical treatment to the walls, they become elegantly assumed into the room's architecture.

*K*nockout knock-th

This room suffered cruelly from a common modern malady—dislocated knockdown syndrome. Though this small urban house was crying out for a big, open living space, I knew it would need help to make it work.

Anyone who's ever knocked down a wall will tell you that the space you're left with after the wall goes will forever be haunted by the fact that it wasn't actually born a nice big room. For a start, there's the left-over stumpy bits of wall support as well as some nasty ceiling scarring caused by that beam you've had to put in to support the floor above. The truth is, left to their own devices and simply painted some timid, pale shade, these rooms can be ugly, uncomfortable, and badly planned. In this space, I've fought hard to seduce the eye and distract the brain into seeing the room as a whole. Bold horizontals from one end to another widen the area, while the mismatched fireplaces appear to be the same size and proportion thanks to panels covered in striped paper and the large television in one balanced by a bronze smoked mirror in the other. A sense of order, balance, and symmetry ensures that your mind doesn't ask itself awkward questions about the exact dimensions it sees. These eye-catching striped fireplace surrounds have been visibly handcuffed together by low shelves that help frame the central section of wall that has been painted a paler shade to show off a large piece of copper wall art. Contrasting color is used to great effect in this room, with pale stone walls receding while striped patterns or solid lamps of chocolatey wood catch the eye and direct attention to where it should be focused.

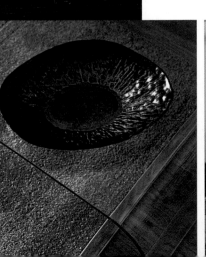

14

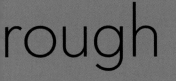

rough

# Using rhythm to right the wrong proportions

There's nothing our poor fevered brains like more than to be soothed by the calming effects of rhythm and symmetry. Our ancient Greek forbears knew this well, hence those regularly placed columns. In a fractured space such as this one, creating symmetry by repeating the same thing once, twice, or three times—whether it's a cushion, chair, or picture—will help to make an awkward, oddly proportioned room feel far more balanced.

## Skirting the issue

In this room, the floor creeps up the wall in lieu of a base-trim treatment. The result is that the narrow space immediately feels that much bigger, as those extra few inches of flooring used as trim end up looking like additional floor space. Simple, but clever.

## Eye spies peacock

Peacock is a rich, sumptuous, heavily indulgent color that can feel horribly cloying when it is used excessively. To ground its exotic flavor, I have applied it in combination with a bitter and powdery black coffee brown. Taking inspiration from the plumage of the peacock himself, acid yellow completes the palette, giving it a citrus back-bite that freshens and cleans up the whole scheme.

## Using the middle rule

Flagging down the eye and dragging it into the center of something distracts it from worrying about the edges. With the hanging of objects, installation of two carpets in the center of the laminate flooring (far left), and through the judicious application of contrasting color, I have used every trick in the decorating book to beguile the eye into believing the space is much bigger than it really is.

My goddaughter—an art student, a DJ, and a part-time volunteer in a local charity shop—wanted to use as little of her allowance as possible to make a space that reflected her interests, her personality, and her belief that "Marie Antoinette rocks."

It started with Sophia Coppola's film *Marie Antoinette*, with its lavish pastel-hued evocation of French ancien régime decadence set to a thumping background of Bow Wow Wow, and ends with this bedroom. Apart from the technicolor-dyed chandelier and the silver gilt plush Louis armchairs (which were birthday presents), everything in this room has been a do-it-yourself project. Stencils, laser transfers, and freehand doodling have all played a part in making the riotous, constantly evolving wallpaper, while the curtains (with a huge helping of help from mom) grew out of studio leftovers I sent over after design collections had been finalized. It's almost as if having been told when a toddler that writing on the walls was out of bounds has inspired her to this ravishing act of aesthetic revenge. This is graffiti at its most glamorous—fusing the raw energy of late 1970s punk rock with the static charm of the late Roccoco. Even the color scheme—a twisted, saccharine version of the revolutionary tricolor's red, white, and blue (here pink, ivory, and Wedgewood)—echoes the punk obsession with defacing tradition. Brimming with ideas, all the elements of this space combine to ask one question: is this teenage bedroom about punking up taste—or tasting up punk?

15

# Post-punk princess

# A sleeping beauty

Here, a traditional wooden bed has been dramatically transformed with a punk-rock Roccoco headboard drawn straight onto the wall. Some studio scraps of wallpaper have been transformed into the "upholstery," while the dark fairytale embellishments are all courtesy of some late-night sessions with a magic marker. As the artist's godfather, I would love to disapprove, but actually I was exactly the same at her age (as indeed was her dad).

## Snug as a bug in a rug

The pale, color-washed floorboards of this room were far too tasteful for such a high-octane scheme as this. Using a stencil and black spray paint, an instant zebra skin rug (opposite bottom left) was created to provide visual impact and break up the wooden expanse.

## Album-cover art

I never thought I'd see the day when the music of my youth hit on trend status again. As a DJ, a finger on the trendy pulse is a prerequisite, but nevertheless it's still a jolt to see one's goddaughter quite so excited by the post-punk vinyl of my own adolescence. Still, these illuminative frames allow classic vintage vinyl to be celebrated as art, while also remaining conveniently accessible should the record in question be worth hearing.

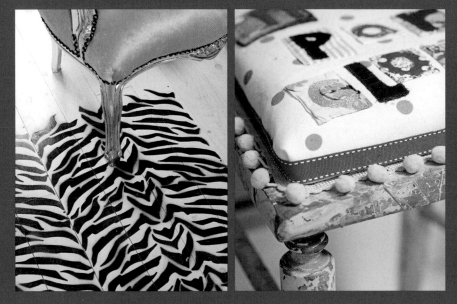

## Never mind Pollock, it's the Sex Pistols

Of all the projects and makeover transformations in this room, I love this chair the most. The seat has been upholstered (courtesy of mom) to look like an exquisitely iced birthday cake. But it's the paint-spattered frame that impresses me the most. There's nothing complicated or contrived about this very simple technique—spattering dribbles of paint in a series of sugary shades over what is actually a very humble junk-shop chair.

# Spring greens

This mouth-wateringly fresh kitchen, with its interconnecting dining room, is as wholesome and refreshing as a lovely salad. An island unit that's more like a life raft keeps everything close at hand in the center of this space.

I really don't like kitchens that look and feel as though they are just for cooking. These days, kitchens are nearly always the backdrop to the majority of family living, and so I love to make them into welcoming, flexible spaces where everyone can feel at home. And that goes for the chef, too—where at all possible, it's so much friendlier not to force whoever is cooking to bend over a pan in a dark corner. Here the cooking apparatus—the cooktop and two ovens—stand solid and proud right in the center of the room. Typical space-hogging kitchen cabinets have instead been replaced with an acreage of zesty wallpaper (which is repeated on the lampshades of the ironwork chandelier that masks the modern ventilation unit), while any storage shortfall has been made up by cabinets on either side of the fireplace and a whole wall of open shelves between the two spaces. It's a soft, romantic scheme that flirts with a few retro references, such as the "poptastic" glossy doors and the hippy-chick-scaled wallpaper repeat. The fossil-specked stone of the toe kick and flagstones provides the perfect practical counterbalance to the lacy, delicate glamour of the wallpaper and the lacquered modernity of the room. Possessing a lovely sense of the old and the new treating each other with mutual respect, this kitchen is an easygoing place that doesn't require control-freak tidiness or terminal house doctoring to keep it looking great.

16

# *A* space of two halves

Rather than even attempt to knock out a wall, I have created a generous paneled opening to connect the kitchen with the dining room. On the kitchen side, painted shelves play host to china and glass that get arranged and rearranged whenever the dishwasher is emptied. In the easygoing dining room, cooking and gardening books and plenty of pictures give the room a constantly lived-in informality, while spring-fresh wallpaper and judiciously placed mirrors help to bounce light around both spaces.

## Why green is great

Green is a real light bouncer—
particularly when it's stuffed full of zingy
yellow as it is here. With white, it's
always fresh and chirpy, but notice how
little red I've let into the color scheme.
Instead, using a similarly toned ozone
blue as the main accent color helps to
prevent the scheme from degenerating
into a rather obvious essay in shades of
traffic light.

## Creating symmetry

With the paneled opening (opposite)
creating an elegant frame, both kitchen
and dining room feel entirely
symmetrical. In reality, the opening isn't
anything as central as it has been made
to look, but it has been balanced and
made to appear symmetrical by the
shelves and objects that surround it.
This gives the space a rewarding sense
of clean-cut architecture that provides a
satisfying contrast with the frilly pattern
of the wallpaper.

## Fabulous finishes

There are some great textures for the
eye to linger over in this relaxed space.
Notice the soft, fudgey stone floor and
the icing sugar-patterned wallpaper. But
my favorite finishing touch is the least
expensive, the doors (above). They
have been made from medium-density
fiberboard (MDF) and then been cut to
size before being marched off to the
local automotive shop, where they got
several coats of tough-as-nails, ultra-
shiny car paint.

Surf-shack sophisticate

This seaside vacation home sits up on the cliffs with a view down to a sea swarming with sun-kissed surfers. As an outpost for beach-time expeditions, this space needed to be cozy but uncluttered, chic but low maintenance—and it had to feel as inside-goes-outside (or outside-goes-inside) as possible.

The starting point for this room was the carpet tiles. Yes, that fabulously contemporary-art area rug is in fact made up of good old-fashioned, high-impact, low-maintenance, throw-anything-at-them carpet tiles. This means, of course, that were some of that post-surf snack to spill and slay a tile there's a box full of willing replacements in the closet. But those "gray pebbles" couldn't be allowed to turn this happy vacation atmosphere drab, hence the gloom-busting pink linen and handful of fuchsia accessories on hand to lighten the mood. Many of the elements of this room have been conceived to be as at home inside as they are on the deck outside the large sliding glass doors. All-weather floor cushions in both spaces, as well as planters designed to look as much like indoor furniture as possible, help soften the transition between outside and indoors. Meanwhile the curvaceous whiplashes of collected driftwood boughs make an excellent, almost Art Nouveau base for a slick, glass coffee table. Part shelter from the elements, part extension of the outdoors, this beach house is a very happy place.

17

# Feeling finely balanced

The exterior of this contemporary building works within its wonderful landscape as it makes modern shapes using natural ingredients, such as wood and slate. Inside, slick, sleek elements are softened by the decorative lines and tactile curves of organic pieces, such as the driftwood coffee table. Meanwhile, both modern and organic elements are brought together and invigorated by a nice, big dollop of raspberry sorbet.

## Fringe benefits

Although the views rock, and indeed there is a lot of rock to be viewed, these glass doors (opposite) could also offer temptation to prying eyes. To counter this, and to take the edge off of that classic goldfish-bowl feel that comes with living in a glass house, I found these perfect window-length fringes. Light and airy, they move in the breeze when the doors are open but fall far short of the horrible claustrophobia that is all too often the result of hanging curtains.

## Gnome front

I really wanted to add an element or two to this scheme that would continue the slightly surreal humor of the giant-scale pebbles on the carpet tiles. Because the budget was tight, I was forbidden from finding costly or high-maintenance knick-knacks, so I marched to the nearest garden center and bought a veritable boy band of gnomes. Nothing fancy—just the cheapest they had. A quick dose of white spray paint was all it took to transform them into *the* talking point for anyone coming for brunch.

## Bench press

Hewn from excitingly wiggly lumps of lumber, this sturdy dining table was sourced locally. Because the area often hosts boisterous groups of teenage surfers of indeterminate number, I did away with chairs and decided on good old-fashioned long benches. This means that far more people can be squeezed around the table, and the dining area still feels uncluttered and open.

◆ *Painting a wall 149* ◆ *Laying laminate flooring 202* ◆ *Laying carpet tiles 204* ◆

I was asked to design this modestly modern marina-side property for a couple who really wanted to squeeze the most out of retirement. Their one request was to make the design as tactile as possible. Getting a room right isn't always just a visual art, there's something wonderful about creating a scheme that seduces the other senses as well. When faced with a particularly modern room, focusing on its touchy-feely potential is a wonderful way of introducing well-behaved pattern and detail.

With loads of light bouncing in from the water just beyond the deck, I could really enhance this scheme with some wonderfully tactile details. To start—and as our couple had mentioned that they had both pretty much given up wearing shoes indoors—I decided to install a leather floor that, thanks to radiant floor heating, would not only feel delightfuly soft underfoot but would also be fabulously warm in the winter. The beautiful cedar tan leather floor tiles I found are a real treat for the feet that will also end up softening further over time. Becoming involved in a new house at an early stage means that particular architectural elements can be seamlessly integrated into your design scheme. On one wall, a contemporary fireplace as well as a concealed flat-screen TV (hidden behind a painting and unveiled at the press of a button) were specified as part of the design, which meant both main focuses of the room could be accommodated within the same visual axis. Moving from a large, traditional family house meant finding new, more modern ways to display a lifetime's collection of things gleaned from extensive travels all over the world. It was an exciting opportunity to revisit a large collection of memory-imbued mementos with a fresh eye.

# Silver surfer's surface

18

# Blue horizon

To draw attention to this high, airy, and light-filled space, I chose a nice, warm blue. There's a lot of yellow in this particular shade, which stops the walls from looking icy when skies are gray. Meanwhile, an extensive palette of traditional tweeds used for pillows and curtains warms the room further and provides a rough contrast to the shine of the leather floor.

## Balancing act

I chose to hang the highlights of a lifetime's art collection as a portfolio grouping, trying to avoid symmetry but achieve a sense of balance. This is a wonderful way of making old art feel contemporary and is best done by trying out various groupings on the floor in front of the wall first. If you want to do the same thing, remember to set a middle line before you begin and then work from left to right.

## Height-adjusted hares

On upturned chunky glass vases, a collection of bouncy bronze hares is given prominence and shown off to full advantage (below). Grouping things at a variety of different heights is a wonderful way of giving smaller objects more emphasis.

## The long and the short of it

The tall, narrow windows lacked prominence, so I papered the surrounding wall in a heavily textured dark brown grass cloth. This not only helps to emphasize the windows but also brings a further natural, tactile note to this very urbane scheme, while hinting at exotic Far Eastern locations.

◆ *Painting a wall 149* ◆ *Applying wallpaper 168-9* ◆ *Hanging a picture 196* ◆

Mrs. de Winter wonde

Anyone who has seen Alfred Hitchcock's film version of Daphne du Maurier's novel *Rebecca* couldn't help but be transfixed by the spectacular sets. Mandalay, the ominously beautiful house of the late Mrs. Rebecca de Winter was the main inspiration for this masterful master bedroom.

Though this large bedroom, originally formed from three smaller rooms, may be set in a seventeenth-century stone manor house, the look is very much luxurious film noir. Eye-catching elements, such as the simple black chiffon bed drapes and the black carpet platform that gives the bed such regal presence, inject the space with lots of elegant drama. The room's intricate layers of entrancing patterns have a foliate femininity, however, thanks to the rigorous color scheme of licorice black, cool oyster, gold, and ruby. Curtains in dull gold satin hint at the haute couture styles of the late 1930s, and the wallpaper print and embroidered throw pillows show a prewar sensibility, when Oriental-inspired floral patterns were the epitome of chic. Inspired directly by the film, eighteenth-century cabinets flank the bed, while hovering above the simplistic black suede-covered headboard, an ornately framed Oriental silk painting of the Goddess of the Moon evokes the elegant femininity of the Art Deco period's predilection for the exotic. This room is a highly charged homage to the sort of powerful feminine glamour British literature, and indeed British cinema, celebrated so elegantly in the 1930s.

19

and

## Closet case

Deep, voraciously hungry closets (bottom) are discreetly underplayed, allowing the floral wallpaper to take center stage. Touch latches mean obvious handles aren't needed, while papering the doors in the same way as the walls before hanging pictures on them means they become invisible. It's a perfect example of the art of "glamouflage."

# Dressing up rooms

When I can't remove a wall but want to open up a space, one of my most reliable tricks is to create an elegantly paneled, generously proportioned door case. Here, the adjacent dressing room—with its black-lacquer furniture and mirrored cabinets, which hint forcefully that this is the lair of a Glamazon—is theatrically framed. The two areas remain distinct but feel airy and open, thanks to the subtly reflective pale-gold-printed paper that pulls them both together.

◆ Applying wallpaper 168-9 ◆ Hanging a picture 196 ◆ Covering a lampshade with wallpaper 234 ◆

## Blurring the edges

Thanks to the black carpet border and the matte-black baseboard, it's almost impossible for the eye to work out where the floor ends and the wall begins. The carpet itself undulates with eye-catching whiplash curves, also ensuring that the attention goes straight to the center of the space and away from its camouflaged edges.

## Ace of shades

Within this refined bedroom, lighting and technology are kept elegant and chic. A modern chandelier (opposite top right) hangs poised over each night table, keeping clutter to a minimum and creating focused beams of light in just the right place for bedtime reading. Taking a little inspiration from a boutique hotel trick, a flat-screen TV and mini bar share a discreet antique book cabinet at the end of the bed (left), perfectly positioned for night-time viewing.

# From lowly to lovely

This ordinary suburban twentieth-century living room has profited immeasurably from the marvelous magic wand of makeover and goes to prove that even the instantly recognizable, spitefully featureless architecture of the last century can be elegantly overcome.

Before I began work on this very beige box, the only thing of note was the interesting architectural salvaged fire surround. The room was dark and almost tunnel-like, and it immediately struck me that this space needed more windows. However, because the budget for the project was microscopic, I forgot about expensive construction and instead installed three mirrors with arched tops that were cut for me by a local shop. Finally, using self-adhering lead strips, I was able to turn these mirrors into glamorous "windows," which double the sense of space in addition to reflecting light back into the room from the real windows on the opposite wall. Spaces like this lack rhythm, so I used one of my favorite techniques—trompe l'oeil—to carve up the wall surfaces into elegant panels with a three-dimensional appearance. The color scheme of pale stone, washed golds, corn, hay, and beige sprang from a venerable pair of good-quality vintage curtains that I came across in a local secondhand shop. The final finishing touch for this room was a "greenhouse" of exotic plants. In fact, they're very convincing fakes but do a fabulous job of bringing this room alive and dissolving the boundary between inside and outdoors.

20

◆ A trompe l'oeil panel 160 ◆Installing a floating shelf 199 ◆ Making a shell mirror frame 233 ◆

## Reflected glory

To prevent the distraction of catching your own eye in the large architectural mirrors, I have used various garden-themed objects to deliberately obscure the areas where your reflection is most likely to appear. It means all the space-enhancing benefits of the mirror are there to be enjoyed without the perpetual distraction of narcissism. And narcissism can be very distracting. Here, I've used plants and plinths, but pictures or clocks can be hung over a mirror to achieve the same effect.

## *Chanson d'armoire*

Created with floating shelves and trompe l'oeil panels that end in the arched tops you often get in French furniture and rustic chateau paneling, this skeletal "armoire" (below; opposite bottom center) provides impact without breaking the bank.

## Feeling touchy

The highlights, low lights, and shadows of a number of natural objects, including this wonderful shell-encrusted mirror (opposite bottom right; below; right), chime elegantly and surreally.

# Come into the garden

Using garden acessories such as topiary shrubs and stone planters indoors is a very efficient way of bringing the outdoors inside and expanding the sense of space in small ground-floor rooms like this one. A garden bench or lead urn on the outside terrace that matches one inside helps to draw the eye and interest beyond the confines of the room itself.

Lofty seaside chic

A contemporary approach to decorating the kitchen/dining space of this eighteenth-century loft near the sea has led to a timeless interior where I absolutely love spending time.

Sometimes there's no point in sprinkling your kitchen willy-nilly throughout a large space. In the short section of this L-shaped space, I've squeezed a convenient kitchen where all the appliances are within arm's reach. This interior is all about balance; the clean-cut lines of the local slate contrast elegantly with the softly billowing blue-gray painted plaster walls, while the lacquer shine of the dark varnished floor reflects the random bird's nest of reused ship beams that hold up the ceiling. The view from the window of gray-blue sea, black granite cliffs, and opaque expanse of milky-white sky is the inspiration behind this room's simple, graphic color scheme. The dark wood of the floor is carried up onto the cabinet's toe-kick area, which means the white-painted kitchen doors appear to float, preventing the look from feeling claustrophobic. And rather than clumsy wall units that can make kitchens look much smaller, a pair of plank-like open shelves enable the stored china and glassware to become part of the decorative scheme. Finally, I painted the knotty, splintery old wood timbers that make up the ceiling beams.

21

# $\mathcal{L}$earning from minimalism

While by nature I couldn't be less sympathetic to minimalism (it's all a bit too rigid and short on laughs), there is something to be said for clean lines and an eagle eye for clutter. Particularly when they are, as here, balanced by soft, romantic textures, such as the curtains that cuddle the windows and the glitzy-glam black Venetian mirror that hangs between those same windows. Oddly, despite the contemporary details, there's something rather formal about this space. The well-proportioned long table made especially to fit the room and the satisfyingly simple modern classic chairs add to the air of restrained grace and favor, while the simple chandelier adds a historic touch. It's the sort of scheme I really enjoy—a little bit modern, a little bit traditional, a little bit country, a little bit rock and roll.

◆ Painting woodwork 150 ◆ Installing a floating shelf 199 ◆ Tongue-and-groove paneling 194 ◆ Hanging a curtain 223 ◆

## Storing in plain sight

For a family-friendly seaside escape, this may seem impressively orderly, but when space is at a premium it's essential that rooms don't get cluttered. Storing in plain sight (right) means there's nowhere for extraneous clutter to hide; it also provides an opportunity to play with decorative compositions of different patterns, textures, and objects.

## Let the air flow

Notice how the furniture throughout this room is very leggy. I wanted to maximize the potential for the light to reflect off of the shiny floor; it's amazing what a difference to the sense of space you can make by choosing deliberately thoroughbred, thin furniture with supermodel legs.

## Interconnecting

The layout is typically organic, and the random progression of spaces is part of the joy of this room, but rigid geometric statements, such as the table (below) and the diagonal-cut sea grass rug, anchor a pretty crazy floor plan.

## Stealing views from other rooms

In this open-plan space, there are some fabulously intriguing glimpsed views from room to room. As a result, I've had a lot of fun taking the kitchen's color scheme and its palette of textures and playing around with them a bit within the other rooms of the loft, such as this sitting area (below), like jazz riffs on an original tune.

# Shopaholic heaven

And so what is the well-dressed room wearing this season? Why, it's whatever you've just taken off and left casually draped over a chair, of course.

Control freaks, with their spic-and-span lives, best look away now because this room not only revels in the fun of clutter but also looks totally wrong when neat and tidy. I've always believed we should all be allowed to surround ourselves with the particular things that bring us pleasure. Here, dresses, shoes, handbags, and feather boas combine to create an engaging, eccentric, and fabulously fashionable scheme. And why not? Who says that our possessions should be tamed through imprisonment in dark closets? This scheme works because the room is treated to the same sort of glamorous pattern palette and sugary color choices as the clothes that have escaped from the wardrobe. Quirky ways of showing off these prized possessions, through the use of mannequins and china figurines, means that the eye is constantly diverted and amused. The sultry, theatrical reflections from the foil-printed wallpaper give an ever-changing cloudy-sky effect as reflections and shadows catch and dance across its shiny surface, creating an open horizon background for the plates of painted birds and boughs, mirrors, and picture frames that cover it. This room has an exuberant "happy hour" atmosphere—part tea-time treat, part vintage cocktail vamp—that oozes amused, and amusing, femininity.

22

# Squeezing in storage

The neat attitude to storage within this space is very much inspired by the mingling of convenience typical of French dressing rooms. A pair of reasonably sized built-in cabinets flank the bed in classically inspired symmetry. Stolen alcoves provide necessary space for lamps and bed-time chick lit while a decorative trim frames the bed to add princess-y prominence in the room.

## Shopping around for style

An eclectic mix of furniture styles—from romantic antique to clean-cut contemporary—keeps pace with the fact that the occupant's wardrobe mingles plush, post-party dresses on the same rail as twenty-first-century techno tailoring. Fusion is a very overused word these days, but I have to admit I did really enjoy fusing such contrasting design styles here to make one whole new boho scheme.

## Yummy dummy

What better way to show off a latest purchase than by displaying it on a recycled dress form or mannequin (above)? Dressed and redressed like life-size Barbies, these objects become fusions of fashion and sculpture within the room.

## Bravo for bling

The decadent sparkle of a great deal of costume jewelry finishes off this scheme perfectly. Rather than stuffed away in a box, favorite pieces are draped on a menagerie of china figurines for a surreal effect.

◆ Applying wallpaper 168-9 ◆ Hanging a picture 196 ◆ Upholstering a headboard 218 ◆ Making a pelmet 220 ◆

Well-mannered manor

Personally, I think it's a little pointless to live in a large house and not indulge yourself with paneling, antlers, large fireplaces, concealed passages, and all the things that such a space demands. But perhaps that's just me.

While this house's great room might have oozed history, thanks to several decades of unsympathetic ownership there was surprisingly little architectural interest here. Apart from the stone fireplace surround, the room itself was a blank (or more accurately, beige) canvas. So, where to start? That the room needed bookcases to house a huge collection was a given. In creating them, I took design inspiration from the bigwigs of history, the taste mongers and style gurus of centuries ago, who were all for covering bookcases in fabrics or hand-painting them in patterns. Covered in the same custom-designed paper as the walls in rich shades of chocolate and orange, the bookshelves were built in wallet-friendly medium-density fiberboard (MDF), as the budget precluded fine wood. The disparate colors and odd sizes of the books they house make for a randomly patterned, ever-changing background to the space. Accessory accents in slippery high-gloss tangerine— such as the eye-catching faux-lacquered console table— bring warm hospitality to the chocolate brown throughout this north-facing room. It's the perfect place for the laser-cut iron lamp bases and shades showing continuous views of Venice. Finally, for practicality's sake, I bordered the pale, sand-colored carpet with rufty tufty brown so that constant journeys in muddy country boots wouldn't make their mark.

23

# Sitting comfortably

For this room, I chose sofas that would be of a comfortable size but not so gigantic that they would dwarf the space. Covered in cozy silk velvet, they're the perfect perch for conversation. The large coffee table is, in fact, an old wooden door (carved with the date 1672, which places it around the age of this part of the house) simply displayed on an inexpensive base covered in a piece of carpet. The panels aren't hugely convenient for putting down items that need to balance on a flat surface, so I've placed a series of lacquer trays, books, and platters to act as safe perches for coffee cups or water glasses.

## Secret history

This room profits enormously from its uninterrupted blocks of displayed books and art, so using guile to cover the tracts of utilities or dull conveniences is one way of preserving the space's bookish character. The large bookcase behind the sofa conceals a spring-hinged panel door—leading to an odd collection of small rooms—over which real book spines have been stuck. Meanwhile, a simple framed map conceals a large flat-screen TV (opposite top).

## Slave to the rhythm

I've drawn attention to the pleasing rhythm created by the four tall windows in this room by using elegant tangerine-lined curtains. Stone shelves turn the radiators into console tables, while bronze mirror panels on which I've hung ornately framed portraits make a knowing nod in the direction of early Georgian decorating, where light was maximized by placing classical "looking glasses" between windows (above).

◆ *Painting a wall 149* ◆ *Applying wallpaper 168-9* ◆ *Hanging a picture 196* ◆ *Hanging a curtain 223* ◆

Pearly queen

Pearls have always been a symbol of femininity. From the sea-born goddess Venus, worshipped by the Ancient Greeks for her voluptuousness, to the courtesans of *fin de siècle* Paris, the pearl radiates luxuriousness, abundance, and multifaceted, multicolored charm.

When you work hard, it's so incredibly important that the "my space" you long for looks the way you've always dreamed it would. Unfortunately, this frankly featureless bedroom, with its corner bed, didn't come close to reflecting either the aspirations or dynamic personality of its inhabitant. To help, I prescribed a contemporary take on the traditional four-poster bed, using dramatically layered curtains at each corner. The bed was inspired by the particular, fugitive shades of gray, ivory, pink, and aubergine that a pearl adopts depending on how it's viewed. It's an extremely sophisticated starting point for a very grown-up bedroom, which requires an assembled palette of silks, matte velvets, and embroidered taffetas to work in glamorous layers. While pearl acts as the color prima ballerina, the corps de ballet has been made up of silver leaf, mirror, black lacquer, and chrome to evoke parallels with the starlets' bedrooms of Hollywood's heyday. This scheme owes a debt to a timeless fantasy of femininity; it's difficult to look at what I've done here and not think "boudoir."

24

# $\mathcal{A}$sian serenity

Chinoiserie, a term to describe the particularly feminine evocation of Asian style, adds another layer of texture here. Many of the patterns owe considerable debt to the free-flowing, organic repeats of classic Asian pattern-making. The blossom-studded boughs embroidered on the taffeta pelmets have a very Eastern feel, while the fabulously expensive-looking wallcovering is not quite what it seems. A silvery printed paper was hung, then stenciled, using off-the-shelf Asian motifs in shades of shell. Doing it yourself means that areas you want to emphasize (such as around pictures) or indeed disguise (such as the room's corners) can receive patterns, while the bulk of the wall remains untouched.

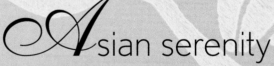

## It's a coverup

I couldn't tolerate anything as everyday as radiators in this fantasy boudoir, so instead I designed these elaborate cases covered in wallpaper with grills and tops silver-leafed, and then shellacked, to look like white gold. Complemented by Roman blinds and pelmets that echo their shape, they become important pieces of furniture in their own right. Meanwhile, the coppery toned, sheer silk curtains serve to hide black-out curtains, which are operated by a remote-controlled, electric track. Now, when morning comes, the black-out curtains part as if on the opening frames of a Hollywood premiere.

## Mix it up

This room is enlivened with elements drawn from many sources. A Victorian-inspired chaise lounge, a distinctly modern dressing table and stool, and a Venetian triptych mirror all chat happily together within this space. Although the periods that inspired all of these things might be different, they are all linked by a strong and very palpable sense of femininity.

Summer living, had me a

This corner room of an old house looks out onto a traditional flower garden. It's the perfect place for summer lunch, so I decided to freeze-frame the moment and decorate this dining room with an "every day is summer" scheme.

Back in the grand old days, people really did have summer rooms, winter rooms, and working rooms—spaces they set aside for a particular time or season. I love this idea, and inspired by the flower borders that sit just beyond the room's windows, I decided to use it here—taking the room outdoors by decorating it with a high-summer pattern. There's something about a classic pattern like this, when used in juicy abundance, that sits well in a room with such restrained detailing. Anything more refined or floral might run the risk of looking pretentious and busybody. Classic French rural decorating inspired the use of a fabric on the tablecloth, curtain edges, and lampshades that complement the wallpaper. For those pattern-phobes who'd worry that a matching tablecloth is a step too far, bear in mind that a repeat this intense really does need an "all or nothing" attitude to make it work. The stiffened edging in the room's main-theme pattern creates frames for the windows, which are finished on top by pelmets covered in matching wallpaper. To give the eye an occasional break, white-painted furniture, a heavy white picture frame, and panels below windows stop the room from getting too shrill or noisy, while the soft, translucent muslin curtains catch the summer breezes and sunbeams, bringing in the outdoors. These touches, combined with the use of simple rustic sea grass on the floor, place the pattern in context and help to create an atmosphere of easygoing, welcoming informality.

25

blast

# Expanding to suit the guest list

Normally set for six, the round table with the glass-topped cloth gets bumped for larger parties. I agonized for weeks about getting the right table—something that extended to sit 10 was required, and proved impossible to find. So instead, folding tables came to the rescue. Here, two oblong tables, under an extraordinarily pretty antique lace cloth, sit in anticipation of a lunch party for 12. Notice, by the way, the duck-egg blue cloth (which is actually a simple bed sheet) grinning through the vintage lace.

◆ *Applying wallpaper 168-9* ◆ *Hanging a picture 196* ◆ *Covering a lampshade with wallpaper 234* ◆ *Making a pelmet 220* ◆

## The enfilade

In France, corridors are treated somewhat with suspicion; I have no idea why. Classic French rooms lead from one to another in a sort of procession that is called an "enfilade." This dining room links the front hall to the kitchen hall, so to minimize the potential ruination brought about by muddy boots and muddier spaniels, a pathway of stone (bordering the seagrass rug that has been laid in the center of the room) extends from hall to hall.

## Indoor/outdoor decoration

A simple formula for keeping this sort of "pattern-tastic" scheme fresh is to break things up with a little white. The lampshades (below), using the same pattern but with a white background, help give the eye a momentary breather.

## Avoiding over-coordination

In a scheme like this—with all its fine finishes, twinkling crystal, and stacked linen—stealing bits of the great outdoors by using flowers and butterfly paperweights (below center and opposite bottom left) helps to echo the wallpaper's motif and makes the room feel like a glamorous picnic.

## Redressing proportions

Windowsills at hip height shout "cottage" loud and clear. This is great if it is cottage you want. I, however, am hooked on long, tall windows with gracious proportions and full-length curtains. Here, I have installed dual panels below each window to give the windows greater elegance and give me an excuse for long, classical drapes.

# Rose-bower burrow

When the going gets tough, the tough get burrowing. While big lofty spaces with iconic views of the city might be modern, they're rarely snug. Here, every trick in the cozy book has been used for country effect.

I've always thought that red and white is the color-combination equivalent of comfort food. It takes you back to an ideal of what home should feel like, be it a real or an imagined sensation. Raspberry pureé high-gloss paint slathered like jam onto breakfast toast provides the perfect background for a variety of shades of white. Thanks to the romantically rustic tongue-and-groove paneling, this room, like the interior of a shiny red shed, is all about comforting enclosure. All the emphasis is on that soft-as-duck-down bed with its heap of pillows, throws, and cuddly blankets, perfect for an aspiring sleeping beauty or princess with a real love of retro. There's nothing here that could be thought of as glam, glitzy, or indeed terribly grown-up, which is what makes it the perfect winter holiday retreat. It also goes to prove that red is one of the most sociable colors you can use when decorating your home. No matter how many shades of it you invite to any party, red is a fabulous mixer and will never ever pick a fight with any of its myriad relations. This bedroom quite emphatically flies in the face of conspicuous consumption; it oozes solid positive values like make-do-and-mend, while proving once and for all that patchwork is definitely the new rock and roll.

26

# Bread and jam

Like windows, the large botanical watercolors in spacey pale mattes and frames float against the brightly colored walls and break up their intensity. The garage-sale-chic collections of furnishings—including patchwork bedspreads reinvented as curtains—also help bring some fresh air into all that steaming raspberry.

## Bewitched by craft

In pattern terms, more really is very, very much more. In this room, shades of white and red are able to unite several dozen different floral patterns—all of which look as though they've got a story to tell about what they were up to before they ended up in this picture-perfect patchwork paradise.

## 360 degrees on the shade

With so much wonderful pattern in this room, I could never have used ordinary lampshades. So instead I created my own. Photographs of the local area, interspaced with scanned-in patterns, were printed onto glossy paper before gluing them over plain lampshades. Now, whenever the light is switched on, the effect created by the patterns is like a patchwork magic lantern show.

◆ Tongue-and-groove paneling 194 ◆ Making a no-sew curtain 221 ◆ Decoupage 228 ◆ Covering a lampshade with tissue paper 235 ◆

## Alice slept here

Playing with scale heightens the fairytale and puts the wonder into Wonderland. Like the botanical pictures, this enormous mirror (above right) also helps to open up the room, breaking up the brightly colored wall and allowing light and space into this red-hued hothouse.

## Rosey supposey

These large roses were painted on the chest of drawers, but they could just as easily have been decoupaged. Notice how painting the chest the same color as the walls has made this potentially bulky piece of furniture retreat quietly into the background.

If there's one thing young children have been specifically programmed to destroy, it's the parental peace of a weekend sleep-in. No matter how boring during the work week, on Saturday morning, they'll be perky and need attention.

This bedroom, with its cleverly integrated bathroom, has been conceived to look coolly chic and perfectly convenient for a bouncy young family. A large flat-screen TV tuned to cartoons in perpetuity, generous leather-covered toy storage, and the convenient bathroom all cater to the boisterous demands of early-riser toddlers. Meanwhile mom and dad can relax in comfortable, monochrome luxury. All that white might at first glance seem very toddler-unfriendly—but all is not quite as it seems. For a start, all the leather in the room is faux, as tough as boots, and very easy to clean. That white shag-pile carpet is actually made up of white shag-pile carpet tiles. So should there be any crayon or juice damage, the offending imperfect tile can be easily replaced from a box of pristine new ones.

# Escaping the parent trap

# Having your minimalist cake and eating it

My task was to reconcile a highly contemporary decorating stance with the practicalities of family living. The all-black tiled bathroom at one end of an all-white room is a wonderfully chic statement that becomes a perfect calming oasis within the hubbub of young family life. This scheme was a matter of parental pride for me. I very much wanted to prove to the young parents of the planet that a designed environment, a space where aesthetics can be integrated along with the diaper bags, is possible and reasonably easy to achieve.

## Peek-a-boo

Rather than put the metaphorical pillow over the head and try to ignore their existence, I wanted the children to feature as an integral part of this scheme. After all, they need to use this space too. As a result, the children pop up everywhere—from the roller blinds to life-size digital-print stickers on the wall—and are reassuringly never out of sight.

◆ *Painting a wall 148* ◆ *Making your own wallpaper with laser transfers 176* ◆ *Mosaic tiling 185* ◆ *Installing a roller blind 222* ◆

## Toy story

The upholstered sleek-lined ottoman that forms the bed's footboard holds all the toys needed to distract these two on a Sunday morning. Notice also how it could effortlessly contain the pair of them—always a good threat. When closed it's the perfect perch for DVD- or TV-viewing in plain parental sight at the end of the bed.

## Tuck-away bathroom

The long and narrow layout of this space meant that a well-appointed bathroom could be squeezed in behind the giant white leather headboard I'd conceived as a room divider. The space continues to feel uninterrupted, and the black tiling in the bathroom serves to emphasize the whiteness of the sleeping area. A seamlessly integrated sliding door does give the option of privacy when needed.

For a lavish, luxurious guest bedroom, I painted the walls to give way to a scenic panorama of idealized parkland. These are my variations on a traditional design theme, playing with the decorating toys Old World aristocrats of another generation so enjoyed.

Much of the cozy, country-house grandeur in this room isn't what it seems. For starters, the proportions of the space itself have been "bent" and "stretched." An unusually high-paneled chair rail increases the feeling of vertical space within the room, while the pair of doors on either side of the bed help to create a sense of balance. One of these is actually a fake, there for just this reason. Odd anomalies in the architecture from the slant of the roof have been camouflaged within the mural, while the large window treatments, with their attention-grabbing, red-lacquered pelmets also distract the eye away from the room's more awkward structural elements, encouraging you instead to see it as symmetrical and pleasingly in proportion. The wonderfully "worn" tapestry used for the curtains and on the bed is actually a highly sophisticated, contemporary digital print of an eighteenth-century French original that has been reproduced on soft linen. It is, if you like, a giant fabric photocopy. Meanwhile, of course, the belief that "red and green should never be seen" is here joyously and unapologetically smashed into a million pieces. This is a room that wallows in the clichés of upper-class decorating confidence, while casually subverting any built-in snobbery with some highly theatrical techniques and a lot of contemporary materials.

(28)

# House-guest heaven

# Red and green *can* sometimes be seen

To paint a vista like this would have been impossible without green, but including it could have led to the typical complementary color fight you get between these two colors—where red acts as a red rag to a green bull. To prevent this, rather than choose the brown-greens that one finds in nature (as you might have expected), I instead chose a strong blue-green. My darkest green then became the color for the woodwork. Having subtly turned the color dial from green toward blue, I then picked a shade of red that errs toward orange. Now with the combative edge having been taken off both colors, both red and green can sit harmoniously together.

## Extra-mural activities

Incorporating some scene-painters' trickery into the design of this mural really helps give the space a sense of open perspective. Vanishing points have been concealed in the corners of the room so that, as one sees the painting from different angles, the rolling landscape appears to behave as a real, three-dimensional view as it unfolds before the eye during a pleasant perambulation.

## Treillage

To keep the chair-rail paneling from looking a bit blank, I designed some Gothic-esque trellises that were laser-cut from thin medium-density fiberboard (MDF) and glued to the wall. This helps continue the Victorian-flavored fiction that stems from the painted landscape.

◆ Painting a wall 149 ◆ Painting woodwork 150 ◆ Upholstering a headboard 218 ◆ Making a pelmet 220 ◆ Hanging a curtain 223 ◆

## What to do with tiny windows

Because the ceiling in the room below this one had previously been raised, the windows here are actually strangely low. To rebalance the funny proportions of this space, I've made a huge theatrical fuss of the curtains, while linen blinds remain permanently lowered to hide the fact that the top of each window is, in reality, below hip height.

There's a fantastical, unusual solution for a family running out of room in the house. Build another one, and then link the two more-or-less identical structures with an open-plan hallway and a vaulted ceiling.

But how do you go about decorating such an extraordinary space? I don't know why I first thought about synthetic grass, but once it was in my brain, it was there to stay. I suppose it had something to do with the fact that this new "room" used to be outdoors. But the practical benefit of fake grass in a high-impact, heavy-use area that offers the main access into the garden is an obvious consideration. The exciting first-floor bridge that links the old and new part of the house had obvious dramatic decorative potential from the outset. I designed an intricate fretwork of bent winter branches to undulate in a rather twiggy, Art Nouveau way from a central corridor landing. After a lot of deliberation, I decided to have the pattern laser cut from grass-green acrylic. When sunlight floods through the glass roof, the translucent balustrade comes brilliantly alive and looks like a magically lit fairy-tale thicket.

(29)

*T*he hallway gallery

# The call of the hall

Obviously, this hallway is much more generous in its proportions than most, so being able to give it uses above and beyond being a straightforward transitional space is easy to envisage. But I'm a great believer in not letting a single cubic inch of a home go to waste. Even in halls a fraction of the size of this one, I will often suggest placing an armchair or an occasional table. OK, not many of us may have a compelling desire to go and sit in a hall, but isn't it nice to have the option should you suddenly feel like it? Anyway, even if you don't have the time to stop and park yourself before you whisk through it, you can have a moment to stop and set your eyes on it on your journey from point A to point B.

## In, out, shake it all about

Tough and practical, but soft and oddly comforting underfoot, the synthetic grass does a fabulous job of giving this interior space an exterior vibe. It also (and here's a serious domestic advantage) looks even better strewn with muddy footprints. But it's not just the floor that's feeling the call of the wild; in this hallway, the walls are clad in the exact same white-painted paneling used to cover the outdoor surfaces. The subtle undulations of shade that light draws out from the wood grain create an ever-shifting pattern, part contemporary design motif, part traditional garden shed.

## Well, hello, Dali!

The surrealism of this space is lost on no one. And it's not just the "lawn" floor, it's things like the floating art and empty picture frames that look as if they're framing a few yards of blank wall. It's no surprise to find ducks in here alongside art featuring repeating gerbils or exquisitely romantic dreamscape landscapes.

Tidy-up time

Remembering back when my two children were tiny, there always seemed to be a power struggle going on for ownership of the living room. Because grown-up spaces quickly become colonized by children's clutter, I had the idea of standing up against the tide of brightly colored plastic by using cunning design to ensure that the living room can regain its grown-up credentials after a three-minute makeover.

This room became the interior design version of the UN, and I was called in to broker peace talks. During the day, Oliver holds sway and takes his responsibilities as messmaker very seriously, indeed. But after bath and bedtime, the living room needs to be a grown-up zone where the responsibilities of child care can be gently eased with white wine and low lighting. While quick, convenient, and easily accessible storage solutions all help enormously, in this scheme my secret weapon for achieving the dual-purpose goal was my choice of colors. The tasteful layering of taupe linens and khakis creates a sophisticated framework onto which I spattered accent areas of bright orange, green, red, and blue. Inspired by the invigorating palette of children's toys, the high-impact color blocks help to soften the impact of kiddie clutter. Using lampshades, accessories, and judiciously chosen art, I fed the room with homeopathic qualities of bright accent color. The careful blend of practicality and style means that there's something in this space for all the family.

30

# Growing up quickly

Yes, it is the same room all grown-up. Thanks to a little help from Oliver, all the toys have now been put to bed in their window-seat storage dormitories, which handily double as additional banquette seating when there are visiting adults. Meanwhile, the chairs have been pulled around a couple of glasses of wine, and the candles in the hearth have been lit. In this atmospheric, sultry light, the room really does feel like an entirely different, far more grown-up place to be.

## Pretty practicality

Practicality doesn't necessarily have to mean sacrificing stylish design. In this room, vertical lines create a visual texture that helps to knit the various colors and themes of this design scheme together. Even the slots of the radiator covers, above, which keep little fingers away from hot surfaces, rhyme. On the floor, a "rug" of carpet tiles is the perfect surface for push cars. And should a cup of juice go awry, the stained tile can simply be lifted away from its companions and replaced with a nice new one.

## Safety first

The dainty lamps on the mantel, right, are plugged into special single-outlet receptacles just below the shelf. They can be controlled by a switch near the door. Placing the receptacles deliberately and discreetly high means that there are no trailing cords for inquisitive little hands to tug. Lighting the room this way as opposed to using floor lamps is another child-proof safety measure.

◆ Painting stripes 159 ◆ Painting woodwork 150 ◆ Hanging a mirror 196 ◆ Laying carpet tiles 204 ◆

# PAINTING

# CLEANING A SURFACE FOR PAINTING

Although, these days, paint has been formulated to go successfully on top of most surfaces, you really don't want dust or muck trapped underneath a permanent top coat. Besides, there's something about preparing a surface for painting that can't help but put you in the right frame of mind for decorating.

1. Mix some trisodium phosphate (TSP) into a bucket of warm water. It's tough stuff, so don't overdo the formulation. TSP is perfect for cutting through paint's archenemy–grease.

2. Use a sponge and some elbow grease to wipe the wall surface you are planning to paint. Start high, and work your way down. This means you won't be dripping onto a clean surface.

3. Make sure the surface is dry before you start any repairing or painting. A dry duster or dishcloth is perfect for getting rid of any excess moisture that may still be on the wall.

# REMOVING LOOSE PAINT OR PLASTER

Loose or crumbling areas of plaster or old paint need to be addressed before you can even think about starting to paint.

1. I always find a wire brush is great for getting rid of surface flakes. Be brave–it's best that anything unstable parts company with the surface at the outset.

2. Now wash the surface down with a water-and-TSP solution to get rid of any dusty leftovers.

3. Abrading the surface will often leave exposed areas of raw plaster that may cause problems later. I'll often use watered-down polyvinyl alcohol (PVA) to seal the deflaked areas.

# FILLING SMALL CRACKS

Modern fillers dry astonishingly fast and can be sanded to an almost invisible state. Spend time applying them well, and you'll save yourself time sanding later.

   (top row images)

1. Always use a putty knife. Fill holes using Spackle or drywall joint compound.

2. Rather like icing a cake, go for swift, maximum coverage at the outset—literally filling the area with little concern for style.

3. Now for the finesse. Positioning the putty knife's edge at a right angle to the surface, scrape off the excess compound from the areas where it's not required.

4. Doing it properly at first should mean there's little to sand afterward. But don't forget, if you're not happy with fix attempt number one, you can always go again until you are.

# FILLING LARGER HOLES

Really scary holes and cracks might need a professional. Big filling jobs require tough love and a make-it-worse-before-making-it-better attitude.

1. Scrape out the damaged area first, ensuring anything loose or unstable bites the dust.

2. Premixed siliconized acrylic caulk is a godsend for these jobs. It's wonderfully flexible and can cover quite significant holes or cracks.

3. Once you've applied a good-enough amount to roughly fill the area, use a putty knife at a right angle to the wall to flatten the rubbery goo.

4. You may find a damp cloth useful to smooth the healing wound off further before it sets for good.

# PAINTING PREPARATION

Painting a room yourself can be good, clean, honest fun. The secret is to relax and enjoy the process. Don't let yourself get anxious or worked up, and whatever you do, for goodness' sake, please don't rush it.

1. It's essential to use well-mixed paint. Have the can shaken at the paint store. I like to start with a good shake—obviously making sure the lid's on tight first!

2. Open the lid with a screwdriver, easing it away gently and making sure you don't bend the lip of the lid back. Little flicks moving gently around the edge are better than a single wrench.

3. Use a paint stick or a wooden spoon to give the paint a good stir. Go on, get right down to the gooey stuff at the bottom of the can.

4. For a water-based paint like this, take a clean, dry, good-quality synthetic-bristle paintbrush, holding its handle just above the ferrules.

5. Dip the brush into the center of the can, ensuring that you don't get any paint on the handle. Load the bristles until they are heavy with paint.

6. Remove the excess. Professional painters pour a small amount of paint into a small bucket. They tap the brush against the side of the bucket to remove excess.

# PAINTING A WALL

I always like to start off painting at eye level. There are plenty who say you should start with the top of the wall or do the "cutting in" (the edges) first, but I like to treat myself to a nice big block of color to get me in the painting mood.

1. Hold your brush gently. If you grasp it too tightly you'll soon tire yourself out, get hideous cramps, and not enjoy the experience. I've always found a loose grip, rather like holding a pencil, works well.

2. Allow the paint to do the work for you. Keep the brush strokes going in energetic crisscrosses until the wall begins to change color.

3. As you go along, make sure you smooth out large blobs or clots of paint, evening out the surface as you go.

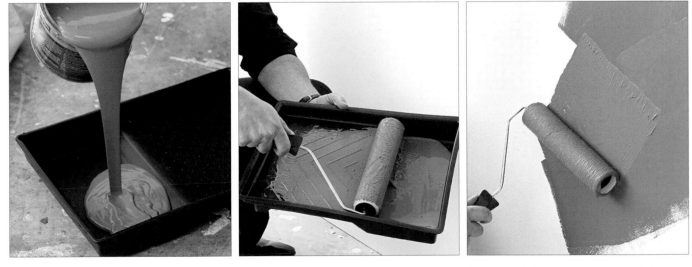

4. When using a roller, start by pouring plenty of paint into the roller-tray reservoir. Then roll an even layer of paint across the surface of the roll-out area.

5. It's important that your roller is as evenly covered with paint as possible. So roll it backward and forward. I'll often give it a couple of passes at right angles just to make sure the color has been spread evenly.

6. Now attack the wall. Beware of the little bits of drying paint or dust that can get stuck in the wet surface. You want the finished surface to be as smooth as possible.

# PAINTING WALL PANELS

There was a time when painting paneled walls or woodwork with smelly, slow-drying oil paints was a fastidious job requiring sanding between coats, patience, and a lot of sighing. Luckily, modern water-based paints make this once-thankless task much, much easier.

1. Assuming you've carefully done all your surface preparation (pages 146-7), start the ball rolling by using a sash brush to paint tight spots and edges.

2. Now attack any panel molding. My tip is to use quite a heavily laden brush to both apply the paint and smooth out the surface as you go.

3. Keep your brush strokes going in the same direction for an equally balanced, consistent finish.

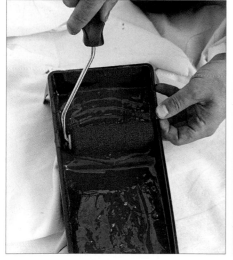

4. Now for the clever part—a small, hard foam roller. This is the best thing I know for creating a smooth, lacquer-like finish. Pour plenty of paint into the tray, and use the roller to spread it.

5. With glossy or eggshell paints, it's extremely important that the paint is uniformly applied to the roller. So take a little time to roll, roll, roll, and re-roll in the roll-out section of the tray.

6. Then go on, making the roller strokes in one direction. Don't even try to do it in one pass. Resign yourself to doing two or three coats to get the best possible finish.

# CLEANING PAINTBRUSHES AND ROLLERS

There are those who go for a disposable-brush regime when decorating—buying them cheap and then chucking them once the job is done. I can't bring myself to do this. I love soft, shiny-bristled paintbrushes and sturdy rollers, and I'm prepared to look after them.

**1.** Clean off as much of the paint as possible using newspaper. I find it has just the right tough-love properties to take off any excess paint cleanly.

**2.** Apply dish-washing liquid straight to the bristles; dip the brush quickly into a bucket of water; and then lather.

**3.** Focus particular attention at the roots of the bristles where the paint can accumulate. For expensive brushes, I might even use conditioner. Rinse and repeat until the water runs clear.

**4.** To clean your roller, start by rolling out the wet paint onto newspaper until there's nothing left.

**5.** Now trickle dish-washing liquid straight onto the roller sleeve before wetting in a bucket of water.

**6.** Beware, rollers are messy!. Treat the roller sleeve like a dangerously muddy dog that's likely to shake everywhere after a bath.

# STORING PAINTBRUSHES AND ROLLERS

There's nothing worse than constantly having to buy things new simply because you can't find (or you hadn't correctly stored) what you already own.

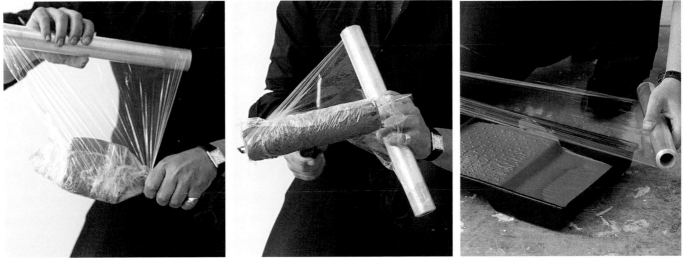

1. To keep a wet brush from getting dry over a lunch break, wrap it snugly in an airtight sheath of plastic wrap.

2. The same goes for roller sleeves. A plastic bag does more or less the same job. Don't leave wrapped rollers or brushes for more than a few hours, however, or they will get dry.

3. Paint already poured into a roller tray can be kept fresh and usable under plastic wrap, too. Be prepared to remove a custard-like skin of paint from the surface if you leave it like this for more than an hour or so.

# STORING A PAINT CAN

When you've got ranks of more or less identical cans stacked in a shed, finding the right color once the label's dropped off can be a nightmare. Try storing them like this to save pain later.

1. I always apply a big patch of paint to the side of the can so that the color is easily visible.

2. Make sure you get that lid back on nice and tight. You should feel a click all the way around as you apply pressure with a hand or by tapping lightly with a hammer.

3. Provided the lid is on properly, I store my paint upside down. This means that the thick coating that forms over the surface of the stored paint occurs at the bottom of the can and at not the top, leaving the paint ready to go when I need it.

# RE-TINTING PAINT

You can use leftover paint—even if it's not the right color. All you have to do is re-tint it. Do the same if the color you bought at the paint store looks too bright when you get it home.

1. Pour one-third of the original shade into a bucket, and set the rest aside.

2. Mix a remedial tint using a suitable acrylic paint. I use complementary color theory to tone down a color I don't like. If a red is too bright, I'll use green, or if a blue is too blue, I'll add orange. But a good catch-all solution is a raw umber, which is a great natural brown.

3. Take a nice big blob of acrylic and mix it with water, being careful to ensure all the undissolved pigment combines with the liquid.

4. Keep stirring until you have a colored suspension with a consistency that could best be described as "gravy-like".

5. Pour the colored suspension into the bucket in which you've put the third of the can of paint. I will usually stir the paint at the same time to ensure an even mix.

6. To assess the change, return a few discreet blobs of the retinted paint onto the surface of the unmixed color. Should your new shade have gone too far, the two-thirds you held back can be called upon to rebalance the mix.

# REMOVING PAINT DRIPS

Accidents happen to the best of us. When they do, swift action is the key—try to soak up as much as possible with an absorbent kitchen towel or newspaper.

1. Dried blobs or spots of paint on the carpet aren't the end of the world. Use a sharp blade to gently scrape them away.

2. Keep the blade at a right angle to the carpet pile, and gently stroke the scalpel-sharp edge over the dried paint.

3. Work slowly and methodically to remove the paint-clogged ends of the carpet pile.

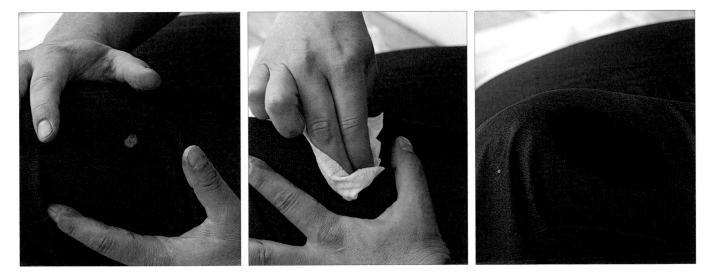

4. On clothes, I've found the most efficient tool in the paint removal armory is the baby wipe.

5. It can take even hardened paint out of the weave of fabric with a consistent, no-nonsense application.

6. With such wonderful paint solvent abilities, I've often wondered whether, after prolonged use, baby wipes might not eventually dissolve babies.

# PAINTING STRIPES

Painting stripes on a wall is, if you like, the bunny hill of decorative paint techniques. Its simplicity, however, is not apparent from the finished effect.

1. Use a spirit level to measure out your stripe lines. I find that it's a good idea to sketch where you want the stripes on a piece of paper first.

2. Use painter's masking tape to create a crisp edge. My tip is to put the edge of the tape on the other side of the pencil line that you have measured to ensure that you paint over the mark.

3. Now take a well-loaded paintbrush, and start filling in the stripes.

4. I always find that painting over the taped edges is best done when the brush has less paint on it. So start painting in the middle first, and leave the edges until last.

5. Leaving tape on for too long can cause problems, so when the paint is dry-ish (about 10 to 15 minutes), peel the tape off carefully.

6. As you get better at this technique, try applying the paint so that the stripes retain a slight brushed texture—which can look wonderful.

# A TROMPE L'OEIL PANEL

A trompe l'oeil panel works best if you pick three closely related shades. When choosing your mid-tone wall color, buy a quart of the darker and lighter shades for just this purpose.

**1.** Using a spirit level and a nice, sharp pencil, mark out your panel, having measured the size, shape, and distance between each side with a measuring tape.

**2.** Use painter's masking tape to mask out the outside edge. If you're really precise, get the edge of the tape so that it leaves the pencil line visible.

**3.** Then mask an inner line approximately ¼ in. away from the outside border. This will be where you'll paint, so having the pencil line between the two tapes ensures that you'll paint over it.

**4.** Neaten up the internal corners with a utility knife. The effect relies on a crisp edge, so make sure there aren't any stray bits of tape.

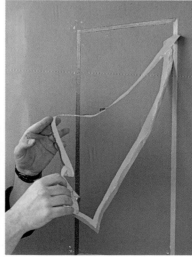

**5.** Look at how the light hits the room. Paint one side and the top in the darker shade to match with what would cast a shadow in real life.

**6.** Use the light color on the opposite side and on the bottom. Where the two colors meet, paint a diagonal line to give the panel that little extra illusion of real depth.

**7.** Peel off the tape slowly. It's a good idea to take off the tape when the paint is dryish—10 to 15 minutes is fine—but not much longer.

**8.** Be prepared to touch up any little areas of damaged paintwork where the tape has pulled off flecks of color.

# MIXING SCUMBLE GLAZE

Scumble is one of decorating's most flavorful words. At its most basic, scumble creates a light, see-through veil of colored paint that takes a long time to dry. There is, however, a lot more fun to be had with scumble, as the following five techniques demonstrate.

1. Pour glaze, in quantities according to the manufacturer's instructions, into a paint bucket.

2. Add either colored latex paint or acrylic pigment into the waiting glaze.

3. Stir well. Remember that the acrylic glaze will appear white when it's wet, so it will make your color glaze look chalky in the bucket.

4. Try it out on your chosen surface and see how it dries before making a final decision. Meanwhile, stir, stir, and stir again to ensure your glaze is thoroughly mixed.

# COLOR WASHING

1. Apply the tinted scumble using a big, soft brush. I always favor a series of large, semicircular strokes.

2. While it's all still wet and gooey, apply more strokes in the opposite direction to build up an abstract, cloudy effect.

3. Now use a soft cotton rag (being careful of unraveling edges, which might get caught in the sticky glaze) to soften the strokes into vaporous patches.

4. When the wall is dry, add further subtlety by sanding lightly. This is also useful if you find dark patches due to paint buildup.

# DRAGGING

Scumbling can create myriad soft, natural-looking textures for bringing a wall to life. Dragging a scumble glaze is a traditional technique that works particularly well in high-ceilinged rooms.

1. Apply a generous amount of tinted scumble in a broad stripe, and brush it evenly to ensure that there are no thick blobs or thin patches.

2. Starting at the top and going down to the bottom, firmly pull an ordinary plastic comb through the gooey glaze.

3. The effect should be of a soft, almost cloth-like vertical texture.

# SPONGING

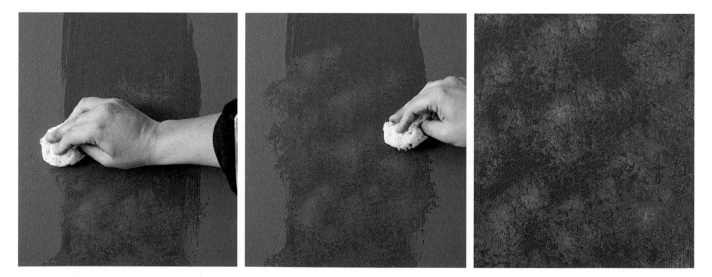

1. Apply the tinted scumble in approximately 12-in.-wide panels, evening out the surface as you go so that it's well distributed.

2. Using a natural sponge, press firmly on the scumble glaze to create pitted blotches that should look a bit like an open-grained wood.

3. A good tip is to constantly turn the sponge—reversing it, swapping it, and rotating it so that you avoid leaving the same obvious impression.

# RAGGING

Ragging is a very old decorative technique that can be traced back to the Renaissance. The imprinted surface creates a fractured, crystalline finish that can look almost marble-like.

**1.** Start by applying a much thicker, even layer of scumble glaze on the wall than you would for the other scumble glaze techniques.

**2.** Take a cotton cloth (being careful of stray threads that might get stuck), and gently leave soft impressions in the wet glaze. Turn the cloth regularly to avoid obvious repeats.

**3.** Alternatively, try using scrunched up polythene bags or plastic wrap in place of the cotton cloth in order to achieve different patterns and effects.

# WOODGRAINING

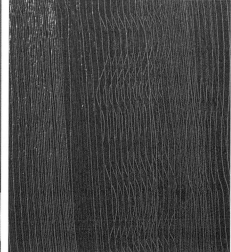

**1.** My technique for simple woodgraining uses a pair of cheap plastic combs. After applying the scumble glaze as you would for dragging, use an ordinary fine-toothed comb to leave delicate vertical lines in the glaze.

**2.** Now use a much broader-toothed comb, such as a wide hair pick, moving it slowly from side to side as you pull down to give a wavy suggestion of woodgrain.

**3.** While the glaze is still wet, you can make the effect more subtle by gently brushing over it in the direction of the grain using a soft, dry paintbrush.

# STENCILING

Stenciling has to be just about the most ancient way of cheering up a surface. The Egyptians were great stencil enthusiasts—as a technique, it suited their taste in repeating patterns perfectly.

**1.** Card stock is the traditional choice stenciling. It's quite thick and smells wonderfully oily. However, I prefer acetate. When cut, it is thin enough to create a crisp stenciled outline. I use non-permanent spray adhesive to hold it in place.

**2.** After giving the stencil a good even squirt, let it dry a bit—it actually gets tackier the longer you leave it—before sticking it to your surface.

**3.** Fixing little squares of masking tape to the corners of the stencil is a good way of making abslutely sure the template doesn't move once you've started working on it.

# STENCILING WITH A BRUSH

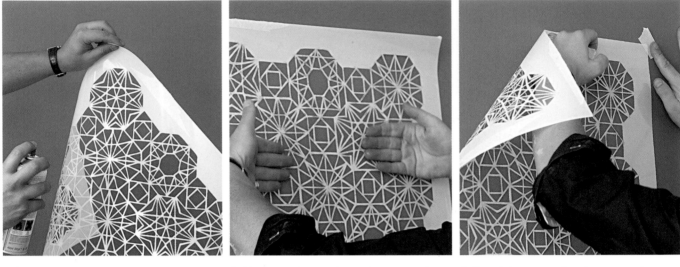

**1.** Using a short, stubby brush, apply a little paint over the open areas of the stencil.

**2.** Try to use as little paint as possible—notice how I've blotted excess paint from the brush onto the uncut part of the stencil.

**3.** When removing the stencil from your surface, peel it off gently, or else you'll risk damaging, ripping, or stretching it.

**4.** To add a sense of depth or volume to the motif, try varying the density of the paint in certain areas.

# STENCILING WITH SPRAY PAINT

Using spray paint has the benefit of providing a more uniform finish than brushing, but the disadvantage is a lot of extra preparation. You'll also need to wear a mask and ventilate the room.

 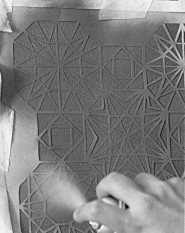  

1. Don't underestimate how far your spray will go. Use newspaper to create a mask around the stencil.

2. Spray your stencil slowly and carefully. Don't blitz the stencil with high-energy blasts of paint. It'll only run if you overdo it.

3. Spray paint dries quickly, so additional colors or (as here) metallics can be added to make decorative effects.

4. This mosaic-style motif looks particularly good with flashes of old gold highlighting the bright pink.

# VARNISH STENCILING

Using a traditional damask motif stencil, you can create your own wallpaper—not with a contrasting or coordinating color, but by bringing in a bit of shine instead.

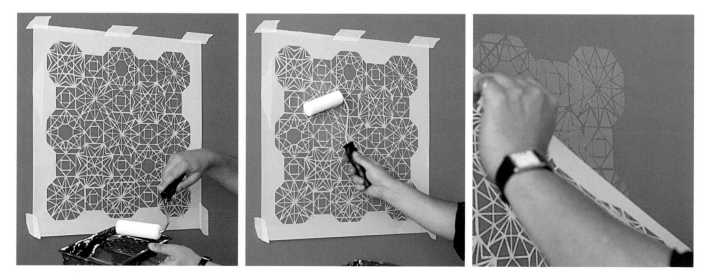

1. Because what you're about to do will take your stencil to its very limits, fix it in place securely before pouring quick-drying gloss acrylic varnish into a small, hard-foam roller tray.

2. Ensure that the roller is not overloaded with varnish but has a nice even coat by rollering it back and forth in the tray. Apply the varnish in gentle passes, regularly changing directions to even it out.

3. Be particularly gentle when removing the varnish-drenched stencil from the wall to avoid smudging or ruining the pattern.

# WALLPAPERING

# APPLYING WALLPAPER

Of all the jobs in the pantheon of decorating, I've always found wallpapering to be the most satisfying. Having said this, it's perfectly normal to view the paper in its tight roll and the wall in its unpapered state with trepidation. Put in the preparation time working out the project first, however, and you will learn to love wallpapering, too.

1. It pays to plan the layout of the strips before you paste. I start in the middle of the wall because I don't trust that the corners are true. (However, some people recommend always starting in a corner. ) Hold up a roll, and mark the edges as your starting points for working across the wall on either side of this middle strip. Using a spirit level, mark the rest of the lines where the other seams will fall.

2. Next, using a dark or mid-tone color from the paper's pattern, paint over each of the vertical seam lines where the paper panels will join.

3. You could color the edge of the roll using a permanent felt-tip marker. This is optional, but it does help if you've got dark, large-patterned paper that might betray itself with a pale paper edge at the seam line when it's on the wall.

4. Measure out your first length of wallpaper. At this stage, it's worth holding the paper in position to work out where the pattern is going to fall. It may even be worth positioning a motif in a particular spot, which you won't be able to do at a later stage.

5. Now cut the one length, allowing almost 1 ft. or so overhang at the top and bottom.

6. I always use a roller to apply paste to unpasted paper. I also roll adhesive directly on the wall; that way, the adhesive is less likely to soak in and create wrinkles or bubbles in the paper. Follow the manufacturer's directions for mixing diluted wallpaper paste for this purpose. Allow the wall to dry almost competely.

**7.** Again using a roller, paste the paper with full-strength adhesive. Get the paste right up to the edges, which is where it is needed most.

**8.** As you go along, fold the paper against itself, adhesive side to adhesive side and pattern side to pattern side (called "booking"), which will give you an easy-to-manage bundle. Then let it stand. I always think in terms of letting a booked bundle stand for the time it takes me to paste the next bundle.

**9.** Now it's sticky time. Be patient at this point. Position the paper at the top, ensuring that the edge follows the vertical spirit-level line on the wall. Gently move the paper using the flats of both your hands until it's more or less where you want it.

**10.** Using a dry wallpaper brush, start brushing down the paper, smoothing out wrinkles and bubbles as you go. Little pouches nearly always dry out on their own, so focus on the big eye-catching imperfections.

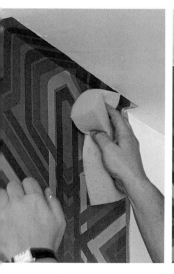   

**11.** Clean off any excess adhesive or fingerprints with a damp, almost-dry sponge.

**12.** Trim away excess paper using a sharp utility knife and a straightedge. Then be brave! When soggy, the wallpaper will look shocking, but—trust me—after about 20 minutes it will look like a perfectly papered wall.

**13.** Match the pattern on your next length of paper. Ensure that you've got an overhang of about 1 ft. at top and bottom before cutting your length to your requirements.

**14.** Cut and paste as before. When positioning the new length, make sure that you match the pattern before you stick it in its final position.

# WALLPAPERING AROUND CORNERS

The current and continuing vogue for papering a single wall is, I believe, something of a missed opportunity. For those who would like to paper further but worry about encountering obstacles, such as corners, let the following reassure you—it's really not that difficult.

1. When you get to a corner, you'll see how important it is not to trust them. Even in newer houses, they're rarely straight.

2. At an outside corner, make sure that the pattern is perfectly aligned and the seam between the lengths is discreetly buffed before attempting to bend the paper. With gentle, horizontal movements, coax the paper over and around the corner.

3. Use a dry brush to get the paper as tight to the corner as possible.

4. Resist the temptation to prod or poke at the paper—at this stage it's most fragile. A soft, dry brush and firm patience work wonders.

5. If the going is getting tough, it's because the paper is getting dry. Keep it a little moist (and therefore pliable) using a damp sponge.

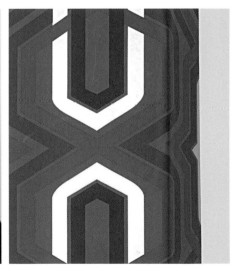

6. I always find that the best finishing touch is a final flourish right down the corner, from top to bottom, with a damp sponge. This makes the paper look crisp and neat.

# WALLPAPERING AROUND A LIGHT SWITCH

Professionals will probably pooh-pooh this, but for safety reasons, I'm not very keen about encouraging anyone to remove a light switch or outlet cover from the wall. Besides, although it may be a little more work, it is actually not a bad idea to learn how to work around intrusive objects.

**1.** Cut your length of wallpaper to fit the wall as before. Then put it up on the wall, as straight as you can, right over the offending switch.

**2.** Now use a pencil to mark the four corners of the switch as accurately as you can.

**3.** Lay the length flat on a work surface, and using a sharp utility knife, cut along the line that would diagonally connect the four pencil marks, stopping about ¾ in. or so before you get to the pencil marks themselves. This allows you a bit of leeway when you install the paper.

**4.** Paste and install the paper as usual. Concentrate on getting the pattern match right and smoothing out bubbles before you begin to worry about the switch.

**5.** Ideally, the cuts you've made in the paper won't completely expose the switch. This means you'll need to trim them.

**6.** To finish, trim away the excess using your utility knife, following the outside edge of the switch.

# COVERING A SHELF WITH WALLPAPER

This is something I like to do a lot. Wallpaper is surprisingly tough and will withstand regular (but not heavy-duty) use as a shelf finish. Papering your shelves to match the wall means that the eye can feast on what the shelves display without the visual distraction of the shelf itself.

1. Use a ready-to-assemble shelf kit. Rough up the factory finish with coarse sandpaper to create "tooth" for the adhesive.

2. Next trace the shelf's outline on the back of the wallpaper, taking care to position the pattern where you will want it to appear on the right side of the shelf.

3. Cut diagonals at each corner to make folding excess paper easier when you apply the paper to the shelf.

4. If it's not prepasted paper, apply heavy-duty adhesive to the back with a roller. Ready-mixed border and repair adhesive is ideally suited to this project.

5. Apply the paper to the shelf, constantly smoothing out wrinkles, lumps, and bumps as you go.

6. Fold the corners in, and then trim off the waste using a sharp utility knife.

7. Use a straightedge with great care and patience to smooth down the paper and ensure that it clings crisply to the shelf.

8. Trim off anything left overlapping on the back edge of the shelf that will butt the wall.

# APPLYING WALLPAPER IN PANELS

Cutting decorative shapes in patterned wallpaper and then applying them in regular intervals onto a wall is a great way to create a grand paneled feeling economically.

1. Draw one-half of a glamorous panel shape on the top of the paper you wish to use, and cut it with a sharp pair of scissors.

2. Fold the paper panel in half down a vertical centerline so that the top edges of the paper coincide in a perfect geometrical line.

3. Trace the profile of the cut shape onto the uncut half of the paper to make a beautifully symmetrical "butterfly" match. Cut out the shape.

4. Apply heavy-duty paste or border and repair adhesive, taking care to get into the corners and over the edges. This is important because the edges of your shape must not easily peel off or be susceptible to damage

5. Apply the wallpaper. Pay particular attention to excess adhesive that might ooze from under the edge and mark the wall.

6. Repeat using the same shape in a careful rhythm. A good tip is to pre-mark a vertical line with a spirit level for each panel position.

# STRIPPING WALLPAPER

Taking down wallpaper is often thought of as an onerous and tricky task. It's not, in fact. The secret is to get between the wall and the wallpaper with as much moisture as possible.

1. I've found over the years that one of the best ways of starting off is to close all the windows and doors and keep boiling an electric kettle or running a humidifier in the room until the steam really builds.

2. Encourage the paper off the wall by gently scoring it using a sharp knife or scoring tool. Be careful not to scratch the surface below. This will help the steam to get in behind the paper.

3. Use either an old-fashioned sponge or a wallpaper steamer to get water or vapor behind the wallpaper through the slashed weak points. The wetter the paper becomes, the easier it is to remove.

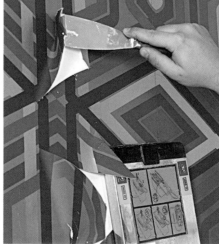

4. Now gently coax small pieces of paper away from the wall using a paint scraper or a flat spatula.

5. Start at the weakest points, such as the joints between panels or at the top or bottom edges of the paper.

6. Don't be greedy. Keep the pieces you scrape off small. Large sections of paper pulled by over-excited fingers may damage the wall.

# MAKING YOUR OWN "WALLPAPER" WITH LASER TRANSFERS

Computers are wonderful tools for a creative person, and I've fallen in love with their ability to print out any motif onto transfer paper, which can then go straight onto the wall—or even onto a throw-pillow cover—as pictured here.

1. Cut around the edge of the printed transfer paper that contains your chosen design, creating a reasonable facsimile of the intended idea of the finished shape. Then position the motif using masking tape.

2. Once happy with the position, lift up your transfer and apply slightly diluted polyvinyl adhesive (PVA) to overlap the shape. If you use a roller, it will be less likely to bubble or dribble.

3. Remove the paper transfer from the wall, and leave the PVA to become tacky but not too dry. Remember that PVA dries clear, so as long as you can still see its opaque whiteness, you're ok.

4. Pop the transfer into a bucket of water, and wait for it to curl into a roll.

5. Now delicately position the transfer on the wall over the tacky PVA, and then slide away the backing paper.

6. Use a dry sponge to flatten out bubbles and, when it's all dry, finish the job by coating the wall with a quick-drying acrylic varnish.

# TILING

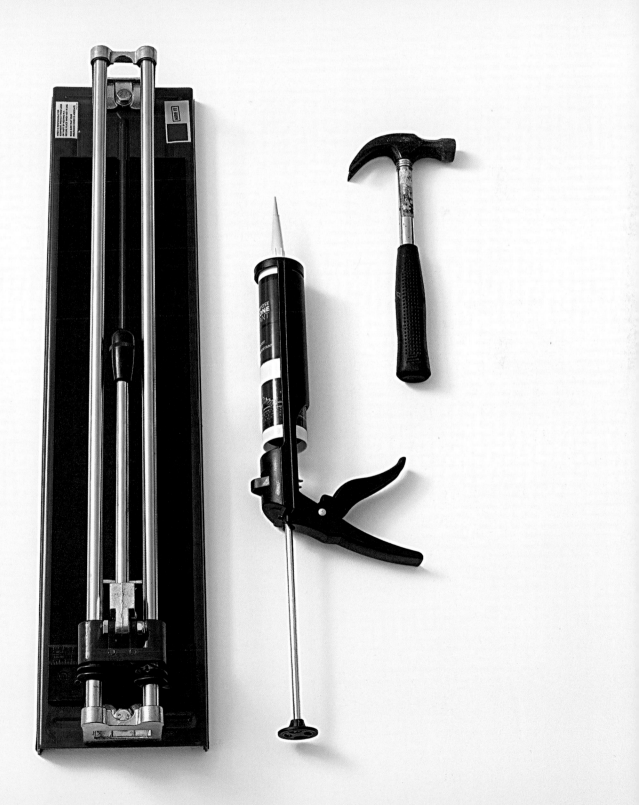

# TILING

Terrible tiling and sloppy grouting can really make bath times a bore. Installing tiles the right way can be very rewarding—an ideal Saturday afternoon job you should be able to finish and let set for a day—in time for a Sunday evening bath treat.

1. Lay out the area you intend to tile. Never trust a corner or a ceiling to be straight. Mark out a vertical centerline in the middle of the tiling area using a spirit level.

2. Now measure how many tiles you'll need for the area you want to cover. Be prepared to add ⅛ in. to each tile dimension to accommodate grout.

3. Lay your first row of tiles along the floor, starting with one in the middle. Its centerline should correspond with the vertical centerline you've marked on the wall. This will also demonstrate where you'll need to cut tiles. It's best to keep tiles that need to be cut in discreet positions in the corners.

4. Now get messy with it. Apply tile adhesive onto the wall in a consistently thick coat. Use a notched trowel to distribute the goo in many lines; this will help the tiles adhere better.

5. Because you're starting from the base molding, snip one limb of the cross-shaped tile spacers.

6. Start tiling, using the spacers you've cut down from crosses into upside down Ts. The spacers are essential for creating a crisp effect, so take time to get them right.

7. Start building up your tiling, course on course, with spacers at every junction between the tiles. Keep checking your tiles with a level to make sure your work is even.

8. Wipe off any adhesive ooze before it has a chance to dry. Now step back, and let the tile adhesive dry thoroughly.

# GROUTING AND CAULKING

At this pregrouted stage your tiling may look a bit ragged, but don't despair. Once the grout and caulk have been applied, it will all look wonderfully professional.

1. Make sure everything is firm before applying premixed grout using enthusiastic scrapes of a rubber-edged trowel. Take time to force the grout into the gaps, and then, keeping the trowel at a right angle to the tiles, scrape off the waste to instantly clean up the look.

2. Now take a semi-damp sponge, and wipe across the tiled area to remove any trace or film of grout from the face of the tiles. Rinse the sponge frequently.

3. Apply silicone caulk to the edges of the tiles. When applying caulk, try to keep consistent pressure on the caulking gun so that the line of silicone remains as free of big blobs as possible.

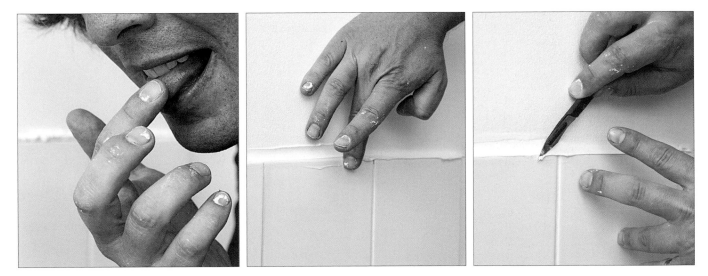

4. To finish and clean up the bead of silicone, there really is no beating a lightly licked finger.

5. Drag your damp digit across the silicone line in one consistent motion to smooth it out and clean off any excess.

6. If finishing the silicone goes slightly awry, don't panic. Simply wait for it to be thoroughly dry before scraping off blotches with a utility knife.

# CUTTING TILE

There is, I must concede, something rather nerve-wracking about cutting tiles to size. Until you gain confidence, I advise making some practice cuts on already-broken tiles.

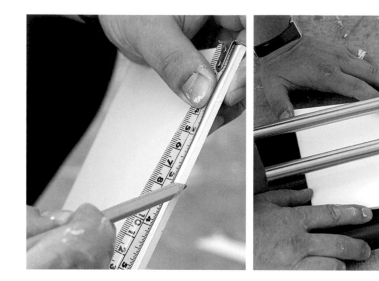

1. Carefully measure where you need to cut your tile. Use a soft pencil to make a mark on the tile's porous, unglazed edge.

2. Position the tile in a tile cutter, making sure that the cutting wheel and your measure mark coincide.

3. Apply pressure to the cutting wheel handle. You'll find that a positioning, steadying aluminum "foot" will come down to fix the tile in place and stop it from wiggling around.

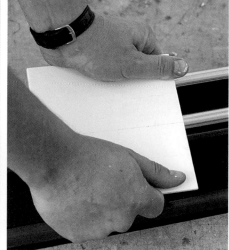

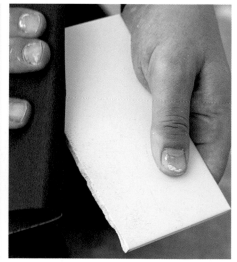

4. Draw the cutting wheel across the tile in one steady pulling motion. Resist the temptation to do this more than once. Honestly, it will work the first time.

5. Now that you have scored the tile, place the weak-point score line over a straightedge, and apply pressure to each side: Presto! Snap!

6. Finish off the raw edge by smoothing it down with some wet/dry sandpaper.

# REMOVING A TILE

When you've got one tile that's cracked, damaged, or just plain ugly, it's not really necessary to condemn the whole wall. This technique will show you how to remove and replace the offending tile, leaving the remainder intact.

1. Using a utility knife or, better yet, a grout saw, score the grout around the tile. Use ordinary masking tape to cover the offending tile from corner to corner.

2. Then, using an electric drill with a carbide bit, drill a hole through the point where the masking tape crosses. Using the masking tape ensures that the drill has something to grab and should prevent it from skidding.

3. Now it's time to shatter the tile under controlled conditions by putting the head of a screwdriver into the center hole and hitting the end using a hammer.

4. Now use the screwdriver to flick out the remaining chunks of the offending tile.

5. Clean the "wound" by scraping off the old dried adhesive and scratching out the raggedy grout.

6. To finish, apply fresh adhesive and install a new, undamaged (or at least marginally better-looking) replacement tile.

# TILING OVER TILE

Tiling over existing tile may be a shortcut, and not necessarily one you should take even if you're in a hurry. However, it can be done—but only on an even surface.

1. Gently scuff the shiny surface of the ceramic tiles using wet/dry abrasive sand paper.

2. Now, as though you were icing a cake, apply a fabulously generous layer of tile adhesive to the gently scuffed tiles.

3. Of course, having tiles on the wall already means that you have a grid system to follow, so you don't really need to mark one out again.

4. Leave the adhesive to set slightly for a few minutes before firmly applying the new tiles.

5. When applying each additional row of tiles, make sure that the spacers are correctly positioned between each tile.

6. Allow the adhesive to dry thoroughly before grouting. Because you have not applied the adhesive over a porous surface, which would ordinarily absorb some moisture, the impervious old tiles will slow the drying time as the moisture in the adhesive evaporates more slowly. Be patient.

# MOSAIC TILING

Mosaic tile is actually quite easy to install. It comes in preassembled sheets with a mesh backing.

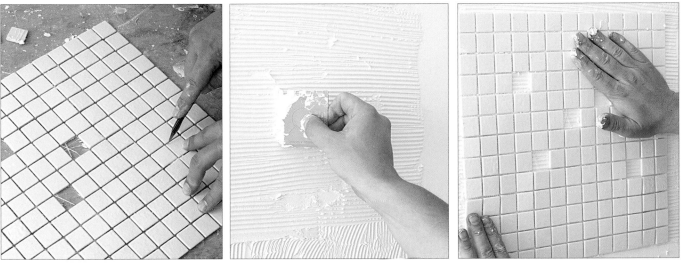

1. Using a sharp utility knife, slit the sheet's mesh backing to pop out a number of individual tiles at random or in a pattern, depending on your design. These individual tiles are called "tesserae."

2. Use a fine-tooth adhesive spreader to apply a thick, even layer of tile adhesive to the surface.

3. Position the mosaic on the surface as you would wallpaper, using the flats of your hands to coax it into position and resisting the temptation to pull, jerk, or tug it.

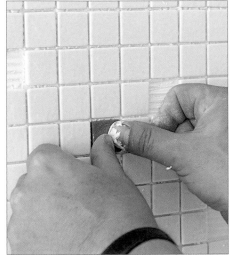

4. Replace the tesserae that have been removed with tiles of contrasting colors or finishes, such as glass or metal.

5. Grout as you would ordinary tile, getting it deep down between each tessera.

6. Finish by wiping excess grout from the tiles' surface using a slightly damp sponge.

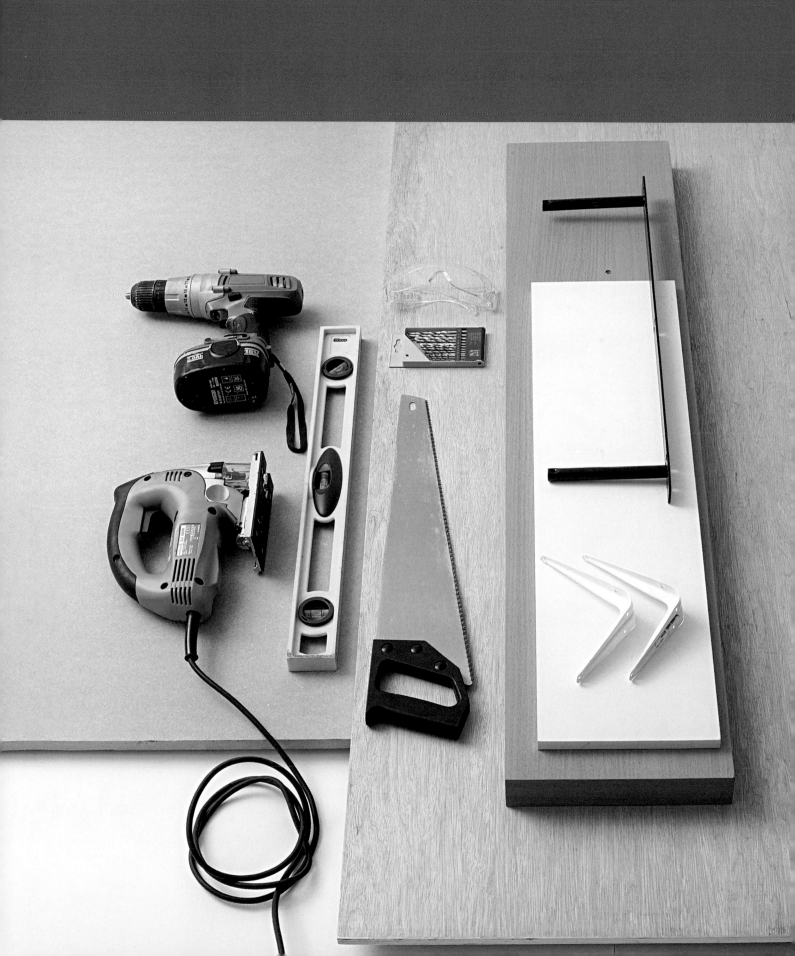

# BASIC NAILING

I've found over the years that there's an almost entirely infallible way of nailing, which I'm happy to guarantee, won't result in bruised thumbs.

1. Hold the nail steady at its very end so that the index finger and thumb create a cushion around the nail's point and the wood.

2. Tap the head of the nail gently but firmly. It helps if you line up the hammer and nailhead by looking straight down the shaft of the nail.

3. When the nail feels securely caught by the wood and unlikely to wobble, hit it home with a circular motion around the nailhead. Resist the temptation to tap, tap, tap directly down. Practice this a few times, and you'll soon get the hang of it.

# BASIC DRILLING AND SCREW DRIVING

There is a whole subspecies of horror films that takes delight in the power tool's potential to maim. Electric and cordless drills are no exception, so be extra careful where you drill.

1. Always make sure your body is fully behind the drill. This will not only help to keep it steady but also allow you a nice clear view of what you're drilling.

2. When you've drilled as far as you need to go, don't take your finger off the button. You'll find it easier to pull out the drill bit while the device is still running.

3. When using a screwdriver, hold the screw firmly in place, ensuring that it goes securely into the wood.

# BASIC SAWING

Cutting wood with a handsaw always looks far more heroic and strenuous than it actually is. Having said this, there is a knack to it—a knack that practice helps and patience perfects.

1. So very practical and handy, the handle of this saw and the straight back edge of the blade create a perfect right angle, making it easy to mark a true line to follow using a pencil.

2. Make sure the board is placed on a secure, wobble-free surface onto which you can also (preferably) place a steadying knee. Watch your fingers, and slowly draw the teeth of the saw over the marked edge.

3. Slowly and rhythmically, draw up the saw, before allowing gravity to pull it down as much as possible. Pushing too heavily or over-pressing the down stroke will force the saw blade to bend, making sawing very heavy going.

# USING A MITER BOX

For narrow, delicate, or decorative moldings or for when you need to cut a miter joint, the miter box and backsaw have a delicate touch.

1. Line up the measured and marked-up molding with the saw gap in the miter box.

2. The backsaw works properly only when it's kept completely horizontal, so resist the temptation to raise the handle as the teeth pass over the molding.

3. For really delicate moldings, place a scrap of wood at the bottom of the miter box to raise it up to a practical level for the cutting teeth of the saw. This will also make the molding less prone to splintering as you cut.

# BASIC CUTTING USING A SABER SAW

The saber saw opens up a whole new horizon of shape cutting, but be careful when operating it as this is one extremely dangerous piece of DIY equipment.

1. Draw the shape you intend to create. My tip is to use a dark, soft pencil so that you'll still be able to see the pencil outline clearly when the dust starts flying.

2. As you plan your cutting, work out in your mind where it will be safe for you to stand, keeping a close eye on where the electric cable is going to be.

3. Make sure the saw is on a slow setting, at least to start with, and you're off! As with power drills, power saws should still be running when you remove them from the wood.

4. For practicality and safety's sake, circular shapes such as this should be drawn as close as possible to the edge of the sheet of wood.

5. Keep your body, hands, fingers, and extremities well behind the saw at all times. You may find that a steadying hand holding the two cut pieces together as you saw helps.

6. You can carefully remove little imperfections after the main event.

# CUTTING DECORATIVE SHAPES WITH A SABER SAW

Creating a decorative shape from a sheet of plywood is a wonderful way of finishing off a screen, mirror frame, or bookcase. As a project, its skill level is way below its considerable design impact.

1. Start with a straight line to mark the center of the symmetrical motif. Then draw half of whatever fancy-pants, curly-wurly design you have in mind.

2. Now cut out this shape as carefully as possible, keeping it in one piece and finishing it along the straight edge of the centerline.

3. Now for the clever part. Use the remnant from this first side as a template for the other side by drawing around it in pencil. This should create a perfectly symmetrical mirror image.

4. Cut around the marked line on this second side as before, keeping a keen eye on safety.

5. For internal patterns, such as this heart, start the ball rolling with a thick drill bit. Drill down just inside the line to be cut.

6. You may find you need two, sometimes three, holes next to each other to create a large-enough slot for the saber saw's blade to fit.

7. Starting from this drilled slot, cut out your shape. You may find you have to reposition the saw a bit in order to get around the entire shape.

8. Clean up any clipped edges or missed turns with the saber saw set on a very slow speed before sanding the edges to finish.

# SANDING

Believe it or not, there is an art to sanding. Doing too little is worse than useless, but going over the top with sandpaper that is too coarse can absolutely ruin a project.

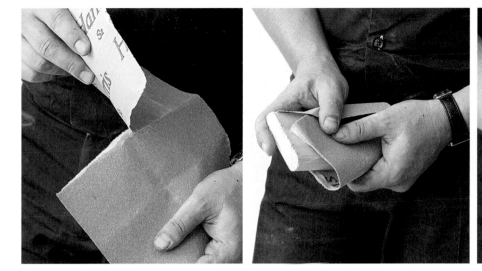

1. I always buy packages of mixed of sandpaper. Coarse paper is great for tough, quick jobs, but you'll need something finer for finessing. Whatever sheet you use, start by tearing it in half.

2. Always wrap your sandpaper around either a store-bought sanding block or piece of lumber.

3. Wrapping the sandpaper around the block not only makes the whole process much less tiring but also, crucially, helps you to control the sanding.

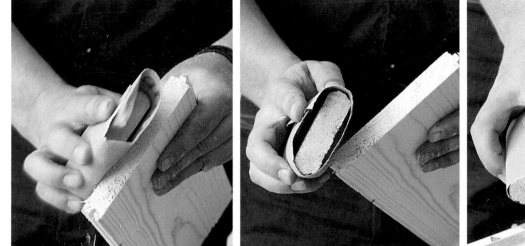

4. Use coarse paper initially to attack big pieces of rough lumber like this, turning the block every now and again so that the paper wears evenly.

5. Now switch to a fine paper to avoid losing the crisp edges of your saw cut to the over-abrasive attentions of heavy-grade papers.

6. As a final touch, gently and evenly sand the edges with a very fine paper until the surface is smooth.

# TONGUE-AND-GROOVE WAINSCOTING

While some experts might tell you that you need to attach tongue-and-groove wainscoting to horizontal furring strips, I've always found gluing it works just as well.

1. To start, you'll need a straight line to follow. Use a spirit level to give you both a vertical line for the first plank and a point for the height of each subsequent plank.

2. Apply paneling adhesive. You'll find plenty of appropriately strong adhesives at your home center or hardware store.

3. Although it's the adhesive that will hold up the planks for posterity, a little paneling nail driven through the plank into the wall will stop any nasty sagging while the glue dries. (Sagging is always bad.)

4. Then—on your mark; get set; go! See how fast you can get around the room. But make sure as you go that every plank you attach is plumb.

5. Finish the whole thing off with molding. Chances are that you could glue it on but, as it might get knocked off, I suggest screwing it in place.

6. Mark where you want to put your screws using your spirit level to ensure that they are level. Now drill through the molding and into the wall. Don't forget to keep the drill turning as you draw it out.

7. Pop in a wall anchor using a willing hammer, and screw the molding to the wall. A diligent carpenter would use a countersink bit when drilling the hole into the molding so that the screw head doesn't protrude.

# WOODEN PANEL MOLDINGS

There's nothing more gracious, elegant, or jaw-droppingly Georgian than a wall decorated with regularly spaced moldings. The project is not as hard as it might look, and if you use a somewhat plain, lightweight molding, you can install it without using screws.

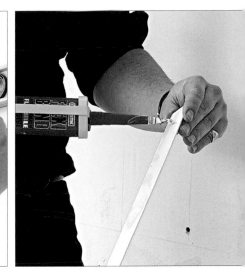

1. Measure the length of your panel molding, and remember to mark the side of the measured line where you'll be cutting your miter.

2. Cut the mitered corner using a tenon saw and miter block. Cut the miter on top of a piece of scrap lumber to hold it in place and keep it from splintering as you finish cutting.

3. Mark out your panel on the wall using a spirit level.

4. Apply a liberal squiggle of panel adhesive all the way down the molding, making sure to keep the edges reasonably free of anything that might squeeze out.

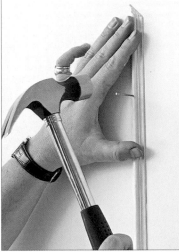

5. Now dull the panel nails you will be using to keep the molding in place while the adhesive dries. Hit the sharp end gently to remove the sharpness from the point.

6. As you drive the nail into the molding, you'll find that by dulling the nail you have substantially reduced the chance of the panel molding's splitting along the line of the nailhole. It really does work, honest.

7. Before attaching the moldings to the wall, lightly sand each corner using fine-grit sand paper. This will finish the joint and get rid of any furry, splintery edges.

8. Continue paneling around the wall until the finished effect begins to resemble a very grand room in a very grand house.

# HANGING A PICTURE

There's a simple rule to hanging pictures: make sure that the bottom of the top one-third of the picture is on exactly the same level as your eye. This is an infallible way of getting the height right.

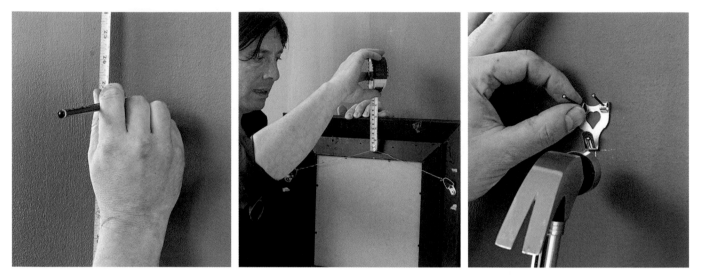

1. Having held the picture up to the wall and decided on its best position, measure where you want the top of the picture frame to be.

2. Now measure the distance between the top of the picture and the taut picture wire as it will be when the picture is hanging.

3. Use a picture hook at the point where you've subtracted the distance of the picture wire from the top of the frame.

# HANGING A MIRROR

Mirrors are surprisingly heavy beasts that are worth attaching properly.

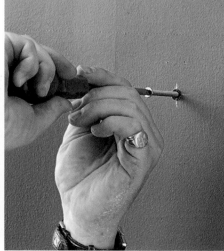

1. First of all, check that there is no possibility of electrical wires behind the wall where you want to drill by avoiding areas near outlets and plugs.

2. Once you have marked your position and drilled into the wall, attach a wall anchor and a screw that is long enough to protrude slightly from the wall.

3. Hang the mirror on the protruding screw. Be gentle and patient because not getting the wire onto the screw properly could lead to disaster.

# HANGING A PICTURE WITH MIRROR PLATES

I like to use mirror plates on ornate frames because they allow the picture to sit flat against a wall. They're also very useful for hanging frames or mirrors on solid doors.

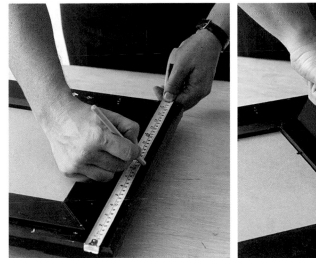

1. Find the midpoint of the picture frame, and clearly mark it on the back at the top and bottom with a pencil.

2. Hold one of the mirror plates in place so that its center point corresponds with the mid mark of the top of the frame.

3. Now use an awl to mark a pair of holes in the wood frame that corresponds with the holes on the mirror plate. Do the same with the other (bottom) one

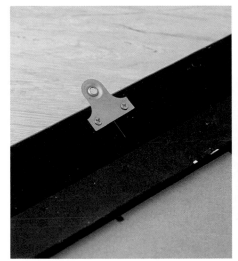

4. Screw the mirror plates to the back of the frame.

5. Position the frame where you intend to hang it, and mark it through the hanging holes of the mirror plates. Finish with screws through the hanging holes.

6. On a door, rather than drilling, you will probably find that an awl will be sufficient to create holes for the screws.

# INSTALLING A BRACKET SHELF

Putting up a shelf is, believe me, satisfying beyond measure. To be able to arrange a few objects on a shelf that you have installed yourself takes house pride to a new level.

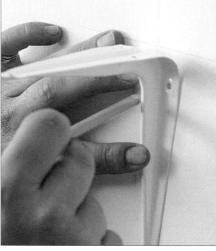

1. First, measure the shelf and work out where you want the brackets to be. Then give yourself a straight line to follow courtesy of a spirit level.

2. Finalize the position of the brackets, and mark out straight vertical lines, which will correspond with the exact centers of the brackets. Hold each bracket up to the wall, lining it up between the vertical and horizontal lines, and then use a pencil to mark the position of the screw holes.

3. Drill the marked holes using a drill bit slightly thicker but not longer than the screws. Don't forget to keep the drill spinning as you take it out.

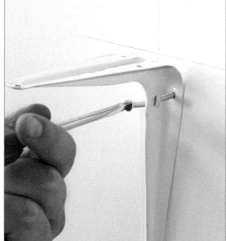

4. If you can't screw directly into a wall stud, pop wall anchors into the holes and use some "tough love" hammering to push them in fully.

5. Hold up each shelf bracket, and screw through the holes and into the plugs behind.

6. To keep the shelf steady, use the holes on the underside of the shelf's support brackets to drill and screw each bracket and shelf together.

# INSTALLING A FLOATING SHELF

Shelves that seem to float on a wall have become extremely popular, with floating shelf kits now available pretty much everywhere. I am one of their most ardent fans, but remember—if you are thinking of installing these shelves, do not overload them . . . or else!

1. Starting off with the assistance of your ever-helpful spirit level, mark out both a horizontal line the length of the shelf as well as a vertical line where you intend the center of the shelf.

2. Hold up the (soon-to-be) concealed bracket to the wall, and mark the exact position of the screw holes with a pencil.

3. Follow the screw-hole marks with a drill—keeping the weight of your body evenly behind it and your eyeline down the bit to create straight holes.

4. Now use wall anchors to fill the holes.

5. Screw the bracket into place. Keep checking to make sure your work is level using a spirit level.

6. Slide the floating shelf onto the prongs of the bracket. Many shelf kits also provide discreet screw holes on the underside so that the shelf can be firmly screwed to the concealed bracket.

# FLOORING

# LAYING LAMINATE FLOORING

When it first hit the scene, laminate flooring was responsible for a decorating revolution. It's easy to see why, as it enables you to easily achieve a wood (or more often wood effect) floor without the protracted hassle of sanding.

1. This floor is going straight onto an unfinished floor. Most laminate flooring requires the use of a foam underlayment as shown here. Check the instructions for the product you use.

2. For some laminate flooring, individual boards simply click together, making installation extremely easy. Other products are glued together. Be prepared to wipe up any glue that squeezes out between the seams.

3. When you are satisifed with the first few rows, start slotting the next boards together, making certain that the tongues and grooves of the planks fit together firmly as you go.

4. You may find that as you work your way across the floor, some boards prove difficult to fit together. If so, try another board, or follow the instructions in Step 5.

5. Every two or three boards, give the whole thing a firm tap to ensure a nice tight fit. Use a block of wood as the battering ram and a hammer as the motivation. Never use a hammer alone, as it will almost certainly split the tongue or groove it hits.

6. Should you need to do it, you'll be pleased to know that cutting laminate flooring to size is easy. Always be very gentle as you start sawing, drawing the teeth of the saw carefully over the fragile tongue.

7. Support the sawn piece with a helping hand to ensure the surface doesn't split when the two pieces separate as you finish sawing.

# LAYING VINYL TILES

Shiny floors are a designer's trick for reflecting light into dark rooms or corridors, and vinyl tiles are perfect for the job. They're easy to lay and easy to cut, making them the perfect flooring to accommodate odd-shaped floor layouts.

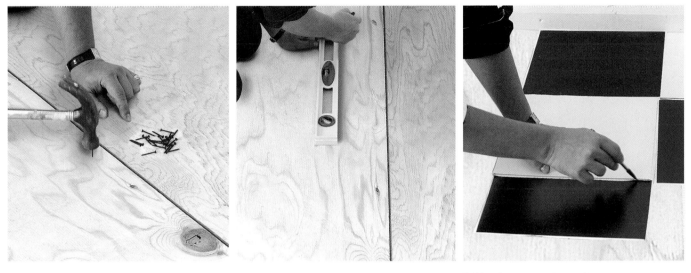

1. Vinyl tiles must be installed on a completely flat, stable surface. Anything else will have to be made level and even before you begin.

2. Before you begin laying your tiles, mark a centerline on your prepared surface. Make sure that your centerline, as here, is visible and can't be mistaken for a joint in the subfloor.

3. Now lay out your tiles in whatever pattern you have decided upon. Here I have chosen a checkerboard pattern of contrasting black and white tiles.

4. When you get to an edge that requires cutting a tile, place it under the tile next to it and mark a line to show where the cut needs to be made. Use a sharp utility knife and a metal square as a guide to make a clean, straight cut.

5. Adhesive-backed tiles fly down, provided the surface to which you want them to stick isn't messy or dusty. Peel off the backing, and get on with it.

6. If your tiles aren't the self-stick variety and need adhesive, spread floor-tile adhesive in evenly distributed squares. The glue should not be so uneven as to affect the smoothness of the surface of the tiles.

# LAYING CARPET TILES

There has been a real, and encouraging, upswing in the popularity of carpet tiles of late, as manufacturers' design teams have started creating products that look every bit the part in the home, rather than in the office.

1. Make yourself a nice, straight centerline to follow in the middle of the room.

2. Now take the first of your tiles, and measure its centerline too.

3. Mark the line clearly on the back side of the tile using a pen.

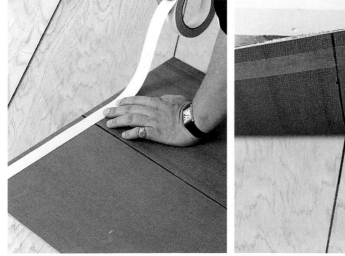

4. If your carpet tiles are not adhesive-backed, attach double-sided flooring tape to the edges on the back of the tile.

5. All carpet tiles have an arrow pointed on the reverse to show you which way the pile or pattern falls. As you go, make sure that the arrows on each tile point in the same direction.

6. Keep the pressure up, and use the palms of your hands to apply the force of your weight to the tile and ensure that the joints between the tiles are as tight and discreet as possible.

# "AGING" NEW FLOORBOARDS

Traditional floors always had a deep, lustrous finish that their proud owners hoped might be mistaken for French polishing. Here is my way of achieving the same effect with new wood boards. But remember, be careful!

1. The best way to bring that old, much-walked-on look to new or recently restored floors is to singe the grain with a hand-held blowtorch.

2. Follow the safety instructions on your blowtorch carefully. Once you have lit the torch, guide the flame across your wooden surface.

3. Use gentle sweeping motions to avoid creating lumpy burned welts on the surface of the grain.

4. Singe the floor slowly and gently, going lightly over areas again and again. You may find that the odd blob of sap in the wood fizzles or stray splinter combusts—but don't panic.

5. At the edges, protect the wall with a piece of flame-retardant-coated plywood or fireproof fabric. Keep a fire extinguisher handy.

6. Remove lose carbonized wood before bringing out the grain using a wire brush.

7. Now apply your wood stain. I find that several coats always provide a wonderfully rich finish that shows off both the color of the wood and its grain.

8. Finally, apply a top coat of non-yellowing polyurethane. If necessary, follow up with a second coat.

# COLOR-WASHING FLOORBOARDS

Treating newly installed or recently refurbished floorboards to a spring-fresh color wash is a classic Scandinavian decorating technique.

1. Start by getting your floorboards wet using water and a large sponge. The wetter the floorboards are, the more open the grain will become, allowing the color wash to penetrate deeply into the wood.

2. Alternate wiping the floorboards with the wet sponge and going over them with a wire brush to create a soggy, abraded surface that will be receptive to the paint.

3. Personally, I tend not to use specially formulated color washes, as I find that standard white latex paint straight from the can and rubbed into the grain works wonderfully.

4. Confine yourself to manageable 3-sq.-ft. blocks. This allows you to concentrate on getting one area right before moving on to the next one.

5. When dry, if the color isn't quite as dense as you would like, repeat the process until you have achieved the desired look.

6. Finally, use a clear, non-yellowing polyurethane over the top to finish. The traditional solution is to wax the colored boards, but I find this quicker, more reliable, and less prone to wear.

# STAINING A BORDER

Inlaid borders of different-color floorboards are a motif of gracious French decorating.
For those with a wood floor who find themselves embarrassed by a lack of luxurious inlay, the
following technique is ideally suited.

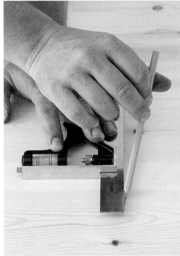

**1.** Check the floor for protruding nail- or screw-heads, and fix them. Then sand the floor, going over it diagonally at first before finishing along the edges.

**2.** Now mark out the border that you intend to stain, using a straightedge and a pencil.

**3.** Using a utility knife, follow both the inside and outside lines of the border. This is essential. The knife scores the grain of the wood, which prevents the stain, when applied, from traveling along the grain and becoming messy.

**4.** Apply masking tape around the edges of your border.

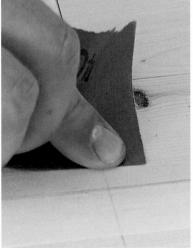

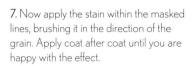

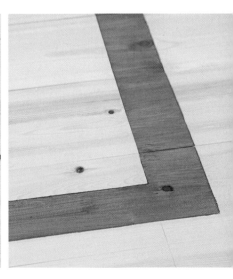

**5.** Use a utility knife to cut the internal corners clear of any stray pieces of masking tape.

**6.** It's very important to remove any pencil marks before the stain seals them for posterity. A light sanding is the best way to do this.

**7.** Now apply the stain within the masked lines, brushing it in the direction of the grain. Apply coat after coat until you are happy with the effect.

**8.** To finish, carefully remove the masking tape. You'll see that the stain has been stopped in its tracks where the grain was cut by the utility knife.

# STENCILING ONTO COLOR-WASHED FLOORBOARDS

Finding a rug to suit a scheme can be a real hassle, so for an economical and highly personal solution, I'll often advocate stenciling your own design.

1. Color-wash the floor for a nice bright background. (See page 208.) Place the stencil, and fix it where needed with non-permanent spray adhesive. Secure the edges firmly in place with masking tape.

2. If you want to create a border around your stencil, simply apply another evenly spaced layer of masking tape around the outside of your motif.

3. Make sure that the floor outside the line of the tape is well protected by plenty of newspaper. Adhere it to the floor with non-permanent spray adhesive.

4. Use spray paint to stencil both the rug and border. I like spray paint because it is extremely tough and will endure well without needing a further top coat. Spray painting is also less likely to stress or damage the stencil than if you used a brush or a roller.

5. Wear a mask as you spray, and open windows to keep the space well ventilated. Use short, gentle bursts of paint rather than long, heavy-duty ones.

6. Let the paint dry. This only takes a few minutes. Then gently remove the newspaper and masking tape.

7. Carefully peel back the stencil to reveal the grand, extremely coordinated effect.

8. Should you want to experiment, try using different colors or a variety of stencil designs to achieve an unlimited number of looks.

# MAKING A CARPET WELL

This technique—the creation of a well within a wooden border in which a carpet may be stretched—is a perennial favorite of mine for tailored, elegant schemes.

1. Mark out where you want your carpet well on the subfloor. Now lay your floorboards. Leave the space that you have set aside for the carpet bare.

2. If you are using floorboards, secure them using nails.

3. Install carpet tack strips to the inside edge of your carpet well. These strips have dozens of sharp barbs protruding from them with a real penchant for pricking stray fingers, so be careful.

4. Cut your carpet piece to size before laying it inside the wood border. Rather than working your way around, it's best to work opposite sides—getting one side in place before immediately heading over to the other side.

5. Carefully coax the raw edge of the carpet onto the tack strip.

6. Finally, use your bodyweight to push the carpet down, impaling the edges onto the tack strip and making sure it's a nice, tight fit.

# SOFT FURNISHINGS

# COVERING A FRAME TO MAKE A FABRIC PANEL

Soft furnishings bring comfort and interest to an interior, and this simple yet highly effective technique makes for the perfect weekend afternoon project. For this particular job, I like to use artist's canvas stretchers, which are available from art supply and craft stores. They come in many different sizes and make the perfect frame for a folding screen or a fabric panel.

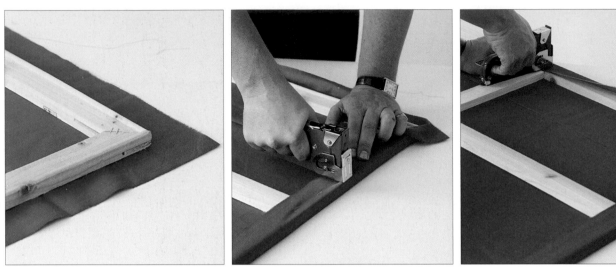

1. Start by cutting your fabric to size before laying it upside down on a flat surface. Now place your frame or artist's canvas stretcher on top.

2. To avoid wrinkles or puckers in the fabric, getting the tension right is important. Pull the fabric tightly around the stretcher before stapling it in the middle of the frame.

3. Now staple the opposite side. This keeps the fabric taut. Finish by stapling the fabric onto the remaining two sides of your frame.

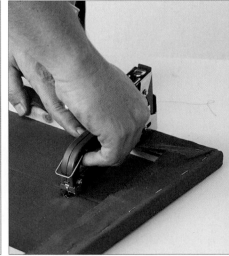

4. At the corners, staple the fabric into the frame's miter joint before folding the corner piece of fabric into a triangle as neatly as you can.

5. Staple through the corner. Repeat this process to finish the remaining three corners.

6. There you have it—a simple panel. If you want to get a bit more advanced, try making a few panels before attaching them together using piano hinges to make a folding screen.

# COVERING A CHAIR CUSHION

For me, there's no point in being able to decorate a room unless you can finish it properly. Obviously, reupholstering a large family sofa is truly a task for a professional, but re-covering the cushion of a dining chair is extremely easy and looks wonderful when done.

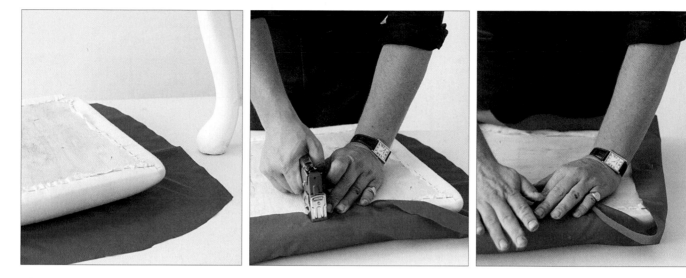

1. Remove the seat from the dining chair, and cut the fabric to size. Allow a generous overhang all the way around to accommodate the rise of the cushion's upholstery.

2. Attach the fabric to the cushion using a staple gun with one staple in the middle of each side. Always work the opposite sides.

3. When fixed at the center of each side, start stapling from the middle toward each corner, pulling the fabric tightly over the cushion.

4. Try to keep the corners as neat as possible. But to be honest, once the cushion is in the chair, the finished effect will be more than impressive enough to hide any small defects.

5. Fabrics that have a slight amount of stretch to them are perfect for this project and will make a nice, neat finish so much easier.

6. All that remains is to place your cushion back in the chair, step back, and admire your work.

# UPHOLSTERING A HEADBOARD

Modern beds can be distinctly lacking in voluptuous drama, so why not try adding a generously upholstered headboard to impart exactly the right balance of soft-comfort glamour.

1. Using a sabre saw, cut a basic headboard shape from plywood. When the shape is cut, use it as a template to trace the shape onto a piece of foam.

2. Cut the foam to shape using a sharp knife. Several upholsterer friends of mine actually swear by bread knives to cut through foam—or even electric carving knives to get through the really thick stuff.

3. Apply permanent spray adhesive or glue generously onto your foam cutout. Foam is absorbent, so you'll find that you'll need several coats.

4. Glue the foam and shaped backboard together; then lay them face down on the fabric.

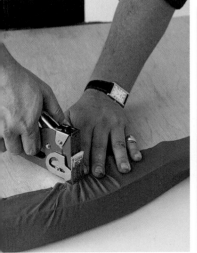

5. Staple the fabric to the back of the headboard. Start in the center of each edge before working around the rest of the headboard.

6. Pay particular attention to corners, keeping the tension on the fabric tight and the pressure on as you staple. I find a few adjustments are essential.

7. A broad, decorative trimming, such as lace or a thick cord, is a wonderful way of finishing off the edges of the headboard, as well as a great opportunity to cover up any little mistakes.

8. Permanent spray adhesive or fabric glue are ideal for keeping edging and trimmings in place.

# MAKING A PELMET

Pelmets are perfect for adding a finished look to curtains on an ugly pole or closing off the space above a blind. There was a time when pelmets were considered old-fashioned, but now they're back with a vengeance.

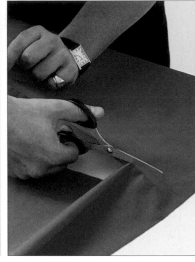

1. Draw or trace your pelmet shape on iron-on fabric interlining before cutting it out. The fabric interlining will keep the pelmet nice and stiff.

2. Draw around the interlining onto the pelmet fabric, leaving a ¼-in. seam allowance.

3. Cut out the fabric shape, paying special attention to the extra that's been left for your seaming.

4. Iron the seams flat. Cut triangles into the corners so that the seams can all be neatly ironed.

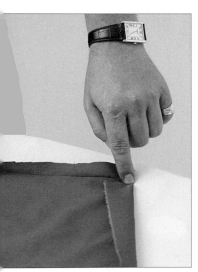

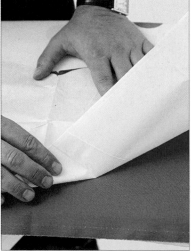

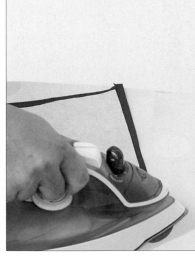

5. As you come to each corner, hold the adjacent seam flat. This will ensure that you don't iron out the seam you've just created.

6. Place the iron-on interlining facedown onto the back of the fabric. It's the rather shiny, slightly adhesive side you'll want to put facedown. Trim off any excess interlining.

7. Iron the back of the interlining. This will activate the glue and bind the lining and fabric together permanently.

8. While it's all still warm and, therefore, not quite set, flip the pelmet over, and iron out any creases on the front to finish.

# MAKING A NO-SEW CURTAIN

A light, cheap, and cheerful window treatment is more than possible without a sewing machine or professional skills.

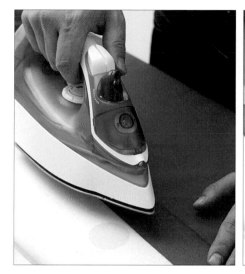

1. Measure, mark, and cut out your chosen fabric to fit the window. Allow enough material for a generous seam at both sides as well as a good 8 in. at both the top and the bottom.

2. Now iron down your seams, giving them a crisp edge. This will make it easy to apply iron-on hemming tape up to the edge of the fold.

3. Take time to ensure that there are no folds or breaks in the tape and that the seam is completely finished. Don't attempt to apply more than a few inches at a time.

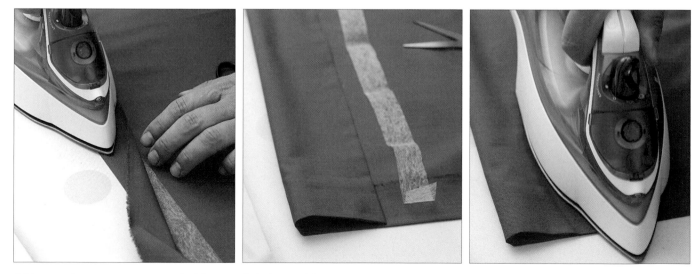

4. Now iron the seam again, ensuring the fabric and tape fuse together permanently.

5. At the top of the curtain, create a pocket for the rod or pole by folding over the 8-in. sleeve before fixing iron-on hemming tape under its lower edge.

6. Iron firmly and flatly. You'll find that simple pocket curtains are extremely easy to make, as well as very useful for finishing a room.

# INSTALLING A ROLLER BLIND

As a quick, easy, and modern window treatment, a roller blind is hard to beat. Roller-blind kits are now widely available and come complete with extremely-easy-to-install instructions.

1. For an outside mount, obtain the width of the frame above the window. For an inside mount, take your measurement from inside the frame.

2. Measure the blind and, if necessary, follow the manufacturer's guidelines to cut it down to size.

3. Using the screws supplied and a drill/driver or a screwdriver, install the end brackets directly into the window frame (outside mount) or inside the frame (inside mount).

4. Pop the blind into the brackets.

# HANGING A CURTAIN

Curtain poles can often be decorative accessories in their own right. Choose one to complement a scheme or to carry through a design theme.

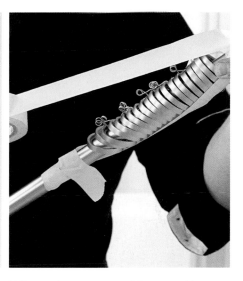

**1.** If your window frames aren't deep enough to allow you to attach the curtain-pole brackets directly, add a piece of 1x4 lumber to the wall above the window using anchors (if necessary) and screws.

**2.** Now screw the curtain pole brackets straight into the wood.

**3.** To stop the curtain rings sliding around (or indeed sliding off) in transit, I always stick them together with masking tape while I install the pole.

**4.** Pop the pole through the waiting support brackets. It will be as you juggle the pole through one bracket and then the other that you will thank me for suggesting that you fix the curtain rings in place.

**5.** Make sure that there's one ring on the outside of the bracket. This means that the outside edge of the curtains will be held in place when they are pulled shut.

**6.** Finish by attaching the curtain to the rings using curtain rings or hooks.

# DECORATIVE TOUCHES

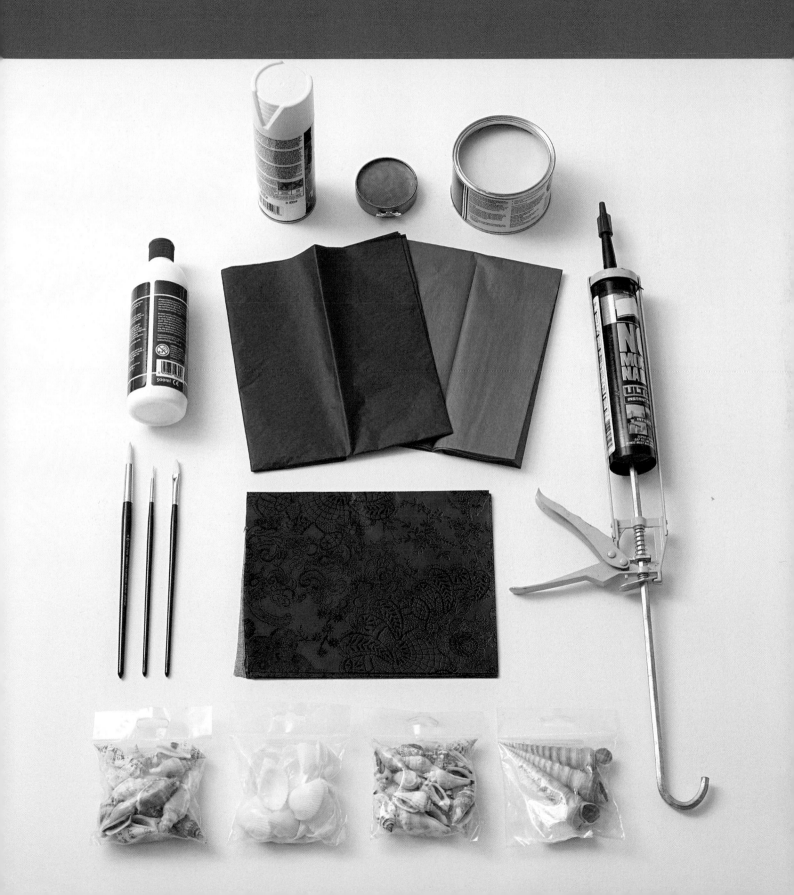

# GESSO WASH

It's important to make a decorating scheme feel comfortable and lived-in by filling it full of bits and pieces that give it a homey touch. Gesso washing is a traditional and very elegant technique for softening a harsh gold finish and achieving an aged look.

1. Start by mixing acrylic varnish with several spoonfuls of gesso, a chalky primer.

2. Paint the solution onto your gilded finish, letting it fill up areas of low relief.

3. Before the varnish dries fully, use a soft rag to wipe off any excess.

# ANTIQUING WASH

Sometimes things just look a little too modern. Giving objects an aged look or a little bit of romantic history is one way of imbuing them with extra character and charm.

1. To create your antiquing wash, mix brown and blue acrylic paint until they become neither true brown nor true blue.

2. To this "gravy," add acrylic varnish until it becomes thick, glossy, and ever-so-slightly transparent.

3. Using a small brush, rub the mixture over the surface you want antiqued. Pay particular attention to areas where age and dirt typically show, and apply the wash only very lightly over edges or corners that would realistically be rubbed and worn.

# GOLD LEAFING

Covering precious objects in gold leaf was a real breakthrough for our ancient forebearers. If you try the following technique, you'll discover how wonderful an experience it still is to take an ordinary object and turn it gold.

1. Traditionally, gold leaf went onto gesso that had been tinted a rust color using red oxide. Personally, I'm more than happy to suggest applying it over red acrylic paint instead.

2. Cover the area to be gilded in acrylic gold-leaf sizing, which goes on white but dries clear. When it has turned clear, blot gold transfer leaf backed on disposable paper onto the surface.

3. Missing bits of gold or little excess flakes of leaf can be correctly repositioned with a dry brush. The idea is to use the leftover gold dust to fill in any bald patches.

# FAKING WHITE GOLD LEAF

White gold leaf was always the cream of the gilding crop. Hollywood divas loved its luxurious glamorous modernity. Needless to say the real thing costs an arm and a leg, but it can be faked.

1. White gold leaf has a characteristic warmth to it, so start off by spraying your object a startling, almost brassy gold. Then spray generously with permanent spray adhesive.

2. Now gently coax loose aluminum leaf (which isn't difficult to track down or expensive to buy) to stick to the sprayed surface using a stiff, dry brush.

3. Use an artist's knife to flick off any stray pieces of leaf and clean up any ragged edges. Then use a dry paintbrush to encourage all the little fragments of leftover leaf to fill in any gaps.

# DECOUPAGE

Decoupage is really just an extraordinarily frilly way of cutting and gluing. Victorian ladies loved to use this particular technique as a way of cheering up their screens or hatboxes.

1. Pick your motifs. Here, extremely old-fashioned colored engravings of traditional roses have been scanned from the computer onto heavy-duty copy paper.

2. Apply a liberal coat of decoupage medium to the back of your desired motif. Make sure to cover to the edges.

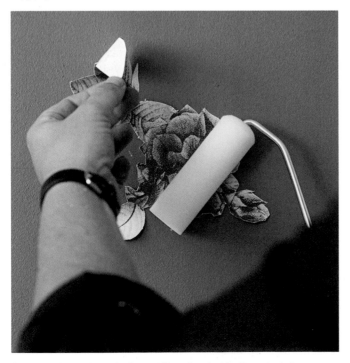

3. I always find a clean, dry foam roller to be ideal for burnishing the cut shapes onto your surface. Start with pressure in the middle of your motif before working your way out to the edges.

4. If you want to intensify the effect, create a repeat using additional images, as here. If you are applying your motif to furniture, finish it by going over it with a top coat of the decoupage medium or a non-yellowing polyurethane.

# "GOLD LEAF" LINING

The Georgians loved to outline painted or lacquered furniture with an elegant line of gold leaf. I've discovered the perfect low-budget, low-tech way of faking it—using a gold marker pen.

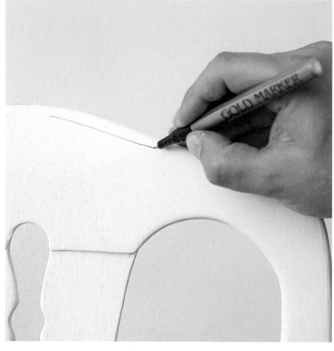

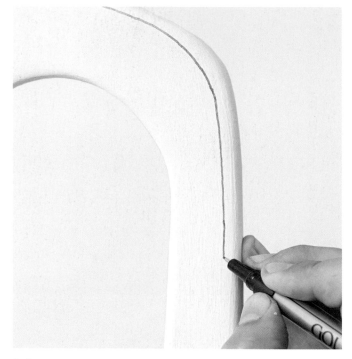

1. If you are applying your gold line to a flat, geometrically unchallenging surface, use a ruler to create a crisp line. For something with a bit of curve to it, use the ring finger of your hand as a guide to follow the shape.

2. Continue your line around the object, touching up any areas that need it as you go.

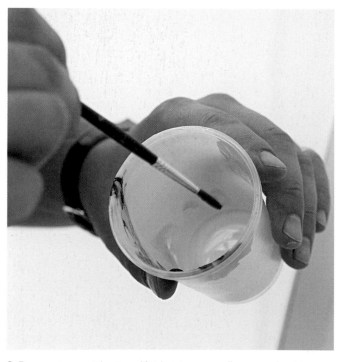

3. For an extra-special antiqued finish, mix up a small amount of antiquing wash. (See page 226.)

4. Apply the wash to "shadow" areas that you have already marked out with the gold pen to darken them and give the finished effect some depth and volume. Traditionally, this is known as "tole work."

# MAKING A SHELL-ENCRUSTED MIRROR FRAME

Shells played a very important part in the history of classical Renaissance and Baroque design. I fell in love with the shell frame designed by Sophy Topley and featured in "From lowly to lovely" (pages 100-103), and I thought I would have a go at making something similar myself. You know what they say about imitation being the sincerest form of flattery.

1. Using an ordinary flat mirror frame in unpainted wood, set out your collection of shells, and then trace around them with a pencil when you're happy with their positioning.

2. Using heavy-duty adhesive, fill the hollows of each shell to be glued.

3. Now, using the outlines as a guide, apply generous dabs of adhesive wherever you intend to place the shells. Then arrange them on the frame.

4. Give the adhesive a good 24 hours to really set before moving the frame onto a surface covered with newspaper. Wearing a mask, spray-paint the mirror frame using your desired color.

5. If you want to retain a little of the color and finish of the shells, you could try applying a gesso wash to them. (See page 226.) If not, then continue spraying in short, even bursts.

6. You may find you need to hold the mirror frame upright to make sure that you get paint into all of the little spaces behind the shells.

# COVERING A LAMP SHADE WITH WALLPAPER

I don't know why people resign themselves to lamp shades that have nothing to recommend them save their neutrality and shading ability. I love lamp shades that bring pattern, color, and luminosity to a room, and this is an easy way of making a boring one do that.

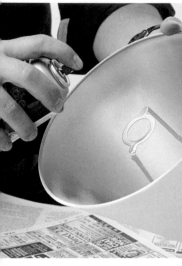

1. Start by spraying the inside of your lamp shade gold to create a wonderful warmth when the light hits it.

2. When the gold is dry, combine several sheets of newspaper to make one large piece that can adequately cover the whole shade.

3. Fix the piece of newspaper in place with tape. Then trim off the excess from the top and bottom using a pair of scissors.

4. When you unwrap the shade, you'll find yourself with a perfectly sized template that is ready for use.

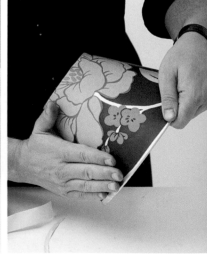

5. Use the template to trace the shape onto a piece of the wallpaper. Make sure you've placed the pattern where you want it to be seen.

6. Now cut out the wallpaper. I like to cut just inside the line so that the wallpaper ends just a little short at the top and bottom of the finished shade.

7. Apply a length or two of double-sided tape to the lamp shade, and then fix the wallpaper in place.

8. When adhering the wallpaper to the shade, try to keep a consistent gap at both the top and bottom to avoid creating a wallpaper "lip" that can be damaged or torn.

# COVERING A LAMP SHADE WITH TISSUE PAPER

You can glue good-quality, printed tissue paper to anything to make an elegant patchwork design. Using tissue papers with contrasting patterns makes for an appealing patchwork effect that will imbue any lamp shade with style and character.

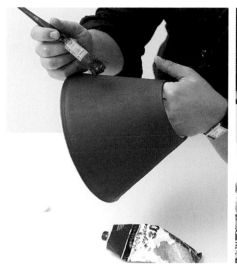

1. Start by painting the outside of your lamp shade with a coordinating-color acrylic paint. This will provide the backdrop for your tissue-paper patterns.

2. Cut the different patterned tissue papers into strips approximately the height of the shade.

3. Using a medium-size brush, apply a liberal coat of polyvinyl alcohol (PVA) adhesive to the shade before sticking the paper pieces on it in relatively random order. Every so often, use the brush to flatten the paper and apply more PVA to the surface.

4. When you have covered the lamp shade completely in paper, cut the edges in a straight line about ¼ in. or so from the edge of the shade. Roll the excess paper over the edge in a neat hem, and glue it.

5. Lastly, apply an additional top coat of PVA to the shade for a tough lacquer shine.

6. Patterned tissue paper can be coaxed over a variety of shaped surfaces. (For added impact, why not try it on your lamp base too?) It can make even the most dull objects look quite special.

# RESOURCES

The following list of manufacturers and suppliers is meant to be a general guide to additional industry and product-related sources. It is not intended as a listing of products and manufacturers represented by the photographs in this book.

## GENERAL

**Acme Sponge & Chamois Co., Inc.**
www.acmesponge.com
Distributes natural-sponge and chamois products worldwide

**Allerdice Building Supplies**
www.allerdice.com
Distributes paint and paint supplies

**Amtico**
www.amtico.com
Manufactures vinyl flooring

**Behr**
www.behr.com
Manufactures paint, varnishes, and related products

**Benjamin Moore & Co.**
www.benjaminmoore.com
Manufactures paint, stains, and varnishes

**Brewster Wallcovering Co.**
www.brewsterwallcovering.com
Manufactures wallpaper, fabrics, and borders

**Calico Corners**
www.calicocorners.com
A national retailer specializing in fabric

**Congoleum Corp.**
www.congoleum.com
Manufactures resilient, high-pressure plastic-laminate flooring

**Cooper Wiring Devices**
www.cooperwiringdevices.com
Manufactures connectors, receptacles, and other wiring devices

**Couristan, Inc.**
www.couristan.com
Manufactures both natural and synthetic carpets and rugs

**Displays2Go**
www.displays2go.com
Manufactures illuminated light frames and light panels

**Dutch Boy**
www.dutchboy.com
Manufactures paint and related products

**Glidden**
www.glidden.com
Manufactures paint and related products

**Grumbacher**
www.grumbacherart.com
Manufactures oil and water-soluble paints

**Home Depot**
www.homedepot.com
A retail source for home-improvement products, hardware, and appliances

**Houston Art, Inc.**
www.houstonart.com
Manufactures metallic powders and other art supplies

**Hunter Douglas, Inc.**
www.hunterdouglas.com
Manufactures shades, blinds, and shutters

**Laticrete International, Inc.**
www.laticrete.com
Manufactures epoxy grout

**Leviton**
www.leviton.com
Manufactures electrical wiring devices

**Loew-Cornell. Inc.**
www.loew-cornell.com
Manufactures artist's brushes and other arti supplies

**Lowe's**
www.lowes.com
A retaile source for home-improvement products, hardware, and appliances

**Magically Magnetic**
www.lyt.com
Manufactures magnetic paint

**Mark James Designs**
www.markjamesdesign.com
Manufactures wall decals

**Minwax**
www.minwax.com
Manufactures wood stains, fillers, and finishes

**Olympic Paints and Stains**
www.olympic.com
Manufactures paints and stains

**Pearl Paint**
www.pearlpaint.com
A retail source for art supplies

**Pergo**
www.pergo.com
Manufactures laminate flooring

**Plaid Industries**
www.plaidonline.com
Manufactures craft-related products

**PPG Pittsburgh Paints**
www.pittsburghpaints.com
Manufactures paints

**Pratt & Lambert**
www.prattandlambert.com
Manufactures paint, stains, and other related products

**Purdy Corp.**
www.purdycorp.com
Manufactures brushes

**Ralph Lauren Home**
www.ralphlaurenhome.com
Manufactures paint and home furnishings

**Seabrook Wallcoverings, Inc.**
www.seabrookwallpaper.com
Manufactures borders and wallcoverings

**Sheffield Bronze Paint**
www.sheffieldbronze.com
Manufactures universal tints

**Sherwin-Williams**
www.sherwin-williams.com
Manufactures paints and finishes

**Solo Horton Brushes, Inc.**
www.solobrushes.com
Manufactures artist's and utility brushes

**3M**
www.3m.com

Manufactures sandpaper, adhesives, and other products

**Valspar Corp.**
www.valspar.com
Manufactures paint, stains, and coatings

**Victoria Larsen**
www.victorialarsen.com
Manufactures stencils and stencil-making supplies

**Wilsonart**
www.wilsonart.com
Manufactures laminate flooring and countertops

**York Wallcovering**
www.yorkwall.com
Manufactures borders and wallcoverings

**Zinsser Co, Inc**
www.zinsser.com
Manufactures wallcovering-removal products, primers, and sealants

## FEATURED AND SUGGESTED SOURCES

**1: Baroque 'n' roll** (p. 24)
www.brintons.net
www.grahambrown.com

**2: The wonder of one** (p. 28)
www.plushpod.com
www.modernica.net

**3: All-natural ingredients** (p. 32)
www.interilife.com
www.aga-ranges.com

**4: Bath night at the opera** (p. 36)
www.grahambrown.com
www.kohler.com
www.vintagetub.com

**5: Living in the closet** (p. 40)
www.furniture-for-small-spaces.com
www.ikea.com

**6: Contemporary cocoon** (p. 44)
www.plushhome.com
www.euromoderno.com

**7: Busy bathroom** (p. 49)
www.seagulllighting.com
www.americanstandard-us.com

**8: A bon viveur bedroom** (p. 52)
www.themagictouchusa.com
www.scandinaviandesigns.com

**9: Retro retread** (p. 56)
www.lecreuset.com
www.vintagelooks.com
www.gomod.com
www.winterbeachmodern.com

**10: Making an entrance** (p. 60)
www.benjaminmoore.com
www.farrow-ball.com

**11: A secret lair with flair** (p. 64)
www.glasstopsdirect.com
www.ballarddesigns.com
www.modernreproductions.com
www.stoneselex.com

**12: Ultra violet** (p. 68)
www.grahambrown.com
www.gascoals.net

**13: Hero of the shower** (p. 72)
www.loccitane.com
www.theinspirationgallery.com
houseofantiquehardware.com

**14: Knockout knock-through** (p. 76)
www.taylighting.com
www.lampsplus.com
www.homedecorators.com
www.modernruby.com

**15: Post-punk princess** (p. 80)
www.etsy.com
www.alibaba.com
www.orientalfurniture.com
www.ballarddesigns.com
www.ebay.com

**16: Spring greens** (p. 84)
www.crateandbarrel.com
wwwkraftmaid.com
www.poen.com
www.corian.com

**17: Surf-shack sophisticate** (p. 88)
www.deroma.com
www.alldriftwoodfurniture.com
www.trendhunter.com

**18: Silver surfer's surface** (p. 92)
www.tjmaxx.com
www.potterybarn.com
www.hunterdouglas.com

**19: Mrs. de Winter wonderland** (p. 96)
www.linensource.com
www.ralphlaurenhome.com
www.shawfloors.com

**20: From lowly to lovely** (p. 100)
www.pillowdecor.com
www.glasstileoasis.com

**21: Lofty seaside chic** (p. 104)
www.qualitycabinets.com
www.benjaminmoore.com

**22: Shopaholic heaven** (p. 108)
www.totalbedroom.com
www.secondhandrose.com

**23: Well-mannered manor** (p. 112)
www.decopatch.com
www.lampshadeshop.com

**24: Pearly queen** (p. 116)
www.simplytablelamps.com
www.restorationhardware.com
www.thibaut.com
www.potterybarn.com

**25: Summer living, had me a blast** (p. 120)
www.linentablecloth.com
www.wallpaperstogo.com

**26: Rose-bower burrow** (p. 124)
www.touchofclass.com
www.ebay.com

**27: Escaping the parent trap** (p. 128)
www.bedsidetables.com
www.kohler.com
www.westelm.com

**28: House-guest heaven** (p. 132)
www.curtainworks.com
www.muralsyourway.com

**29: The hallway gallery** (p. 136)
www.homegallerystores.com
www.astroturf.com

**30: Tidy-up time** (p. 140)
www.homereserve.com

# INDEX

contrast in, 12-13
layout, 11
rhythm in, 12, 78, 115
size, improving of, 10
symmetry in, 12, 70-1, 87

## S

safety, electrical, 143
sanding, 193
sawing, 189-92
screens, covering, 216
screw driving, 188
sculptures, 45
scumble glaze, 161-3
sealing, 146
shelves
    bracket, installing, 198
    floating, installing, 199
    wallpapering, 113, 172
shower room, 72-5
silicone, 181
skirting, 10, 74, 78, 99
sofas, 46
soft furnishings, 27, 43, 55
    chair cushion, covering, 217
    curtains, hanging, 223
    curtains, no-sew, 221
    cushions, 27, 42, 55
    headboard, upholstering, 218
    pelmets, 220
    roller blind, installing, 222
    screen, covering, 216
sound camouflage, 59
space, 10-11, 16, 107
    and color, 15
    and lighting, 18
Space Age chic 31
sponging, 162
spray paint stenciling, 165
stenciling, 81, 118, 164-5
    with a brush, 164
    onto floorboards, 211
    with spray paint, 165
    with varnish, 165
storage, 21, 51, 98, 107, 110, 131, 142
stripes, 10, 41-22, 77
    painting, 158-9
sunflowers, 31
symmetry, 12, 70-1, 77, 78, 87

## T

tapestry, 132
televisions, 20, 92, 99, 11
tiles
    carpet, laying, 205
    cutting, 182
    grouting, 181
    marking out and applying, 180
    mosaic, 185
    removing, 183
    tiling over tiles, 184
    vinyl, laying, 203
to-do list, 6

tongue-and-groove paneling, 125, 194
trompe l'oeil, 74, 160
treillage, 134

## U

utilities, 20-1

## V

varnish stenciling, 165
ventilation, 9
vinyl tiles, laying, 203

## W

wallpaper, 69
    checkered, 73-5
    making your own, 176
    using old in new design, 60-1, 63
wallpapering
    applying, 168-9
    around corners, 170
    a lamp shade, 234
    around light switches, 171
    in panels, 174
    shelves, 172-3
    stripping off old paper, 175
walls
    feature, 13
    motifs, 31, 55, 118, 130
    painting of, 149
    see also wallpaper; wallpapering
washes, 226
windows
    small, 135
    tall and narrow, 97
wine labels, 35
woodgraining, 163
wood-panel moldings, 123, 194
woodworking
    basic cutting with a sabersaw, 190
    drilling/driving screws, 188
    nailing, 188
    painting, 150
    sanding, 193
    sawing, 189
    tongue-and-groove paneling, 125, 194
    using a miterbox, 189
    wood panel moldings, 123, 194

## AUTHOR'S ACKNOWLEDGMENTS

Special thanks go to Anne Furniss, Helen Lewis, Gabriella Le Grazie, Simon Davis and all the team at Quadrille. Thanks also to Polly Wreford and Carolyn Barber for their sumptuous photography.

This book would not have come together without all the wonderful people who opened their doors and allowed me into their beautiful homes. Thanks to Ed and Faye Bowen, Jon and Jules Silver, Tim and Zoe Bawtree, Kate and Paul Kessling, Mark and Donna Kraven, Steve and Davina Clift and Sean and Faye Hodgson, and to all at GL50, The Lower Mill Estate, the Watermark Club, the Bay in Talland, and to Ursala and the team at Urban Splash.

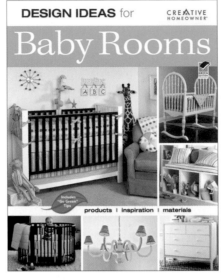
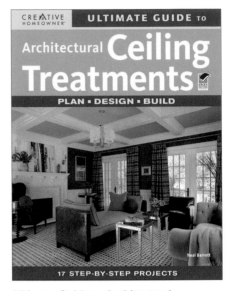
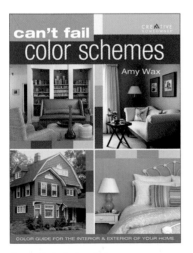
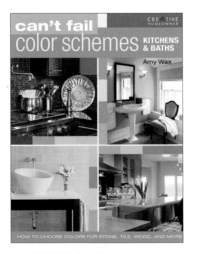